Jacob Ward

The Secret God Who Challenged Christ
A Journey to the Heart of Mithraism

Original Title: O Deus Secreto que Desafiou Cristo

Copyright © 2025, published by Luiz Antonio dos Santos ME.

This book is a non-fiction work that explores the ancient cult of Mithraism, its rituals, beliefs, and its historical competition with Christianity. Through an in-depth analysis, the author examines how Mithraism influenced Roman society and its enduring legacy in Western thought.

1st Edition
Production Team
Author: Jacob Ward
Editor: Luiz Santos
Cover: Studios Booklas / Ethan Harper
Consultant: Marcus Lowell
Researchers: Julia Bennett, Adrian Clarke, Thomas Reed
Typesetting: Oliver Hayes
Translation: Nathaniel Fisher

Publication and Identification
The Secret God Who Challenged Christ
Booklas, 2025
Categories: History / Religion / Comparative Mythology
DDC: 292.07 - **CDU:** 2-47

All rights reserved to:
Luiz Antonio dos Santos ME / Booklas
No part of this book may be reproduced, stored in a retrieval system, or transmitted by any means—electronic, mechanical, photocopying, recording, or otherwise—without prior and express authorization from the copyright holder.

Summary

Sistematic Index 5
Prologue 11
Chapter 1 Unveiling the Mysterious Cult 15
Chapter 3 The Origins of Mithras 25
Chapter 4 From the Frontiers to the Heart of the Empire 30
Chapter 5 Mithras and the Roman Army 35
Chapter 6 The Social Diversity of Mithraism 40
Chapter 7 The Tauroctony and the Birth of Mithras 45
Chapter 8 The Life Cycle of Mithras 50
Chapter 9 The Universe in Seven Spheres 55
Chapter 10 The Mithraic Pantheon 60
Chapter 11 Fundamental Principles and Beliefs 65
Chapter 12 The Path of the Initiate 70
Chapter 13 The Sacred Cave and the Ritual Space 76
Chapter 14 Initiation and the Mithraic Grades 82
Chapter 15 Secret Rituals 88
Chapter 16 Communion and Fraternity 94
Chapter 17 Expressions of Devotion 100
Chapter 18 Visual Language of the Cult 106
Chapter 19 Strength, Sacrifice, and Renewal 112
Chapter 20 The Cosmos in the Mithraeum 118
Chapter 21 Symbolism of Light and Darkness 124
Chapter 22 Other Symbolic Animals in Mithraism 131
Chapter 23 Symbolism of Ritual Objects 139

Chapter 24 The Rise of Christianity in the Roman Empire 146
Chapter 25 Mithraism and Christianity 152
Chapter 26 Mithraism versus Christianity in the Quest for Followers 160
Chapter 27 The Gradual Decline of Mithraism 167
Chapter 28 The Enduring Legacy of Mithraism 173
Epilogue 178

Sistematic Index

Chapter 1: Unveiling the Mysterious Cult - Introduces the modern-day resurgence of interest in alternative spiritualities and sets the stage for the exploration of Mithraism within its historical context.

Chapter 2: The Setting of the Roman Empire - Delves into the unique characteristics of the Roman Empire, such as its cultural and religious diversity, that allowed for the emergence and flourishing of new religions like Mithraism.

Chapter 3: The Origins of Mithras - Explores the enigmatic origins of Mithras, tracing possible connections to Persian and Indo-Iranian traditions while highlighting the ongoing academic debate surrounding its precise roots.

Chapter 4: From the Frontiers to the Heart of the Empire - Traces the remarkable geographical expansion of Mithraism throughout the Roman Empire, driven by military movements, trade routes, and the dissemination of Roman culture.

Chapter 5: Mithras and the Roman Army - Examines the deep connection between Mithraism and the Roman army, explaining how the cult's values and practices resonated with the military ethos and the experiences of Roman soldiers.

Chapter 6: The Social Diversity of Mithraism - Challenges the notion of Mithraism as solely a soldier's religion, highlighting its appeal across diverse social strata in Roman society, including merchants, civil servants, and even slaves.

Chapter 7: The Tauroctony and the Birth of Mithras - Focuses on the central myth of Mithraism, the Tauroctony, analyzing the symbolism of the bull sacrifice and exploring the myth of Mithras' birth from a rock, emphasizing the extraordinary nature of the deity.

Chapter 8: The Life Cycle of Mithras - Expands the narrative beyond the Tauroctony, exploring the broader life cycle of Mithras, including his miraculous birth, heroic deeds, pact with the Sun, and final ascension to the celestial realm.

Chapter 9: The Universe in Seven Spheres - Delves into the elaborate cosmology of Mithraism, focusing on the concept of the seven planetary spheres and their spiritual significance, explaining the soul's journey through these spheres after death.

Chapter 10: The Mithraic Pantheon - Introduces the auxiliary deities and symbolic figures that populate the Mithraic pantheon, such as Cautes and Cautopates, Sol Invictus, and others, revealing the complexity and richness of the divine hierarchy in Mithraism.

Chapter 11: Fundamental Principles and Beliefs - Examines the core theological principles of Mithraism, including cosmic dualism, the quest for salvation, the immortality of the soul, and the rigorous ethical code that guided the conduct of initiates.

Chapter 12: The Path of the Initiate - Explores the practical application of Mithraic theology in the ethical and moral system of the cult, outlining the fundamental virtues and moral principles that shaped the "path of the initiate" and their spiritual journey.

Chapter 13: The Sacred Cave and the Ritual Space - Focuses on the Mithraeum, the distinctive place of worship, analyzing its architecture, symbolism, and ritual function, emphasizing the importance of the sacred cave as a microcosm of the universe and a space for spiritual transformation.

Chapter 14: Initiation and the Mithraic Grades - Delves into the initiatory system of Mithraism, describing the seven hierarchical grades and their associated symbols and rituals, highlighting the gradual and transformative nature of the initiatory journey.

Chapter 15: Secret Rituals - Explores the secret rituals that formed the core of Mithraic religious practice, discussing initiation rituals, sacred banquets, and other possible ritual actions, emphasizing the importance of secrecy and the transformative power of ritual experience.

Chapter 16: Communion and Fraternity - Examines the role of ritual meals and sacred banquets in Mithraism, emphasizing their importance for strengthening community ties, promoting fraternity among initiates, and offering symbolic communion with the divine.

Chapter 17: Expressions of Devotion - Explores the possible verbal and performative expressions of devotion in Mithraism, including hymns, prayers, invocations, and ritual gestures, highlighting the emotional, aesthetic, and communicative dimension of the cult's liturgy.

Chapter 18: Visual Language of the Cult - Analyzes the importance of art and iconography in Mithraism, emphasizing the communicative power of images in conveying myths, theological principles, and esoteric messages, and shaping the religious experience of initiates.

Chapter 19: Strength, Sacrifice, and Renewal - Delves into the symbolism of the bull in Mithraism, exploring its multiple layers of meaning, including primal strength, fertility, sacrifice, death, and cyclical renewal of life, emphasizing the bull's central role in the Tauroctony and the cult's message.

Chapter 20: The Cosmos in the Mithraeum - Focuses on the omnipresence of zodiacal symbolism in Mithraic art and architecture, analyzing the meaning of the zodiacal signs, their relationship to Mithraic cosmology and astrology, and their function in transforming the mithraeum into a microcosm of the universe.

Chapter 21: Symbolism of Light and Darkness - Explores the visual expression of cosmic dualism in Mithraism through the symbolism of light and darkness, analyzing its representation in the architecture of the mithraea, ritual lighting, iconography, and the figures of Cautes and Cautopates, emphasizing the ethical and soteriological dimension of this dualism.

Chapter 22: Other Symbolic Animals in Mithraism - Complements the analysis of the Mithraic symbolic bestiary, exploring the symbolism of other recurring animals, such as the lion, serpent, scorpion, and raven, revealing their multiple layers of meaning and their contribution to the visual language of the cult.

Chapter 23: Symbolism of Ritual Objects - Analyzes the ritual objects that played a crucial role in Mithraic ceremonies, such as the knife, torch, chalice, and paterae, exploring their symbolism, ritual function, and importance in the material culture and religious experience of the cult.

Chapter 24: The Rise of Christianity in the Roman Empire - Contextualizes the decline of Mithraism by examining the rise of Christianity as a dominant religion, analyzing the factors that contributed to its success and the challenges it posed to Mithraism and other pagan cults.

Chapter 25: Mithraism and Christianity - Compares and contrasts Mithraism and Christianity, highlighting their similarities in terms of spiritual needs and religious expression, but also emphasizing the crucial differences that determined their divergent historical paths.

Chapter 26: Mithraism versus Christianity in the Quest for Followers - Explores the religious competition between Mithraism and Christianity, analyzing the strategies used by each cult to attract followers, the factors that influenced this dynamic, and the impact of this competition on the fate of each religion.

Chapter 27: The Gradual Decline of Mithraism - Examines the causes and factors that contributed to the gradual decline and disappearance of Mithraism, highlighting the role of the rise of Christianity, imperial support, religious intolerance, and structural limitations of the cult itself.

Chapter 28: The Enduring Legacy of Mithraism - Reflects on the enduring legacy of Mithraism, highlighting its iconographic heritage, its importance for understanding mystery cults, its presence in popular imagination, and the continuity of scientific research on the cult, reaffirming its historical and cultural relevance.

Prologue

At the dawn of the 4th century, the Roman Empire, once a bastion of power and splendor, found itself in the midst of a profound existential crisis. The old certainties that had sustained Roman society for centuries were crumbling under the weight of civil wars, barbarian invasions, and a growing disillusionment with the traditional gods. Amid this maelstrom of uncertainty, a new spiritual force emerged, offering solace, hope, and the promise of salvation: Christianity.

But Christianity was not alone in its rise. A mysterious cult, known as Mithraism, also flourished in the Roman Empire, competing side-by-side with Christianity for the soul of the Empire. Mithraism, with its roots in ancient Persian traditions and Greco-Roman mysteries, offered a rich tapestry of myths, symbols, and rituals, promising its initiates a journey of spiritual transformation and union with the divine.

At the center of the Mithraic cult resided the enigmatic figure of Mithras, a bull-slaying god, born from the rock and destined to perform the primordial sacrifice that ensured cosmic order and the renewal of life. The initiates of Mithraism, gathered in sacred underground caves, celebrated the mysteries of Mithras through secret rites, sacred banquets, and a gradual progression through seven hierarchical grades, seeking spiritual enlightenment and salvation.

Mithraism and Christianity, although sharing some superficial similarities, such as the promise of salvation and the practice of ritual meals, represented fundamentally different religious paths. Mithraism, with its emphasis on strength, discipline, and the ascent of the soul through the planetary spheres, offered an ideal of moral and spiritual perfection based on self-control and overcoming challenges. Christianity, on the other hand, focused on the figure of Jesus Christ, preaching love, forgiveness, and divine grace as the path to salvation.

The competition between Mithraism and Christianity shaped the religious landscape of the Roman Empire during the 2nd and 3rd centuries AD. Both cults vied for the same faithful, especially among the military, merchants, and the urban middle classes, offering alternative answers to the same spiritual and existential needs.

The fate of Mithraism and Christianity, however, would be dramatically altered by the decision of Emperor Constantine to convert to Christianity and make it the official religion of the Roman Empire in the 4th century AD. From that moment on, Christianity, supported by imperial power, expanded rapidly, while Mithraism and other pagan religions were gradually marginalized and repressed.

The decline of Mithraism was gradual but inexorable. Anti-pagan imperial legislation, growing religious intolerance, and the loss of social and military support undermined the foundations of the cult, leading to the abandonment of its sanctuaries and the disappearance of its rites. By the end of Antiquity, Mithraism had almost completely vanished from the religious landscape, leaving only archaeological and iconographic vestiges as testimony to its existence.

But the legacy of Mithraism did not completely die out. Its rich iconography, with the emblematic scene of the Tauroctony, the cosmic symbols, and the symbolic bestiary, continues to fascinate and intrigue scholars and artists, inspiring contemporary interpretations and recreations. Mithraism, even in its disappearance, left an indelible mark on the history of religion and Western culture, challenging us to unravel its mysteries and understand its subtle but persistent influence on our imagination.

What if history had taken a different course? What if Constantine, instead of Christianity, had opted for Mithraism as the official religion of the Roman Empire? What would the world be like today if the bull-slaying god, and not the crucified Christ, had become the dominant symbol of Western faith?

This work, "The Secret God Who Challenged Christ," invites you on a fascinating journey to the heart of Mithraism, exploring its mysteries, unraveling its symbols, and revealing its complex relationship with Christianity. As we delve into the depths of this enigmatic cult, we are confronted not only with an alternative history of religion but also with profound questions about the nature of faith, the search for transcendence, and the role of power and politics in the construction of history.

Join us on this journey of discovery and be captivated by the mysteries of the secret god who challenged Christ and who, even in his silence, continues to question us through the centuries.
Luiz Santos
Editor

Chapter 1
Unveiling the Mysterious Cult

At the dawn of the 21st century, in an increasingly globalized and secularized world, we observe an intriguing phenomenon: the persistent and, in many cases, growing search for spirituality and religiosity. Paradoxically, amid unprecedented scientific and technological advances, and a massive dissemination of information, many individuals are attracted to spiritual paths that transcend traditional and dogmatic religions. There is a thirst for authentic experiences, for belief systems that resonate with individuality and that offer a sense of belonging in a world perceived as increasingly fragmented and uncertain. In this context, interest in ancient religions, mystery cults, and alternative spiritual traditions flourishes, driven by the promise of ancestral wisdom and transformative practices that can fill the existential void of modernity.

It is within this vibrant tapestry of contemporary spiritual seeking that the fascination with Mithraism arises, a cult that flourished in the Roman Empire, competing side by side with nascent Christianity, but which, to a large extent, remained in the shadow of history, shrouded in mystery and secrecy. For the modern reader, saturated with conventional religious narratives, Mithraism presents itself as an intriguing alternative, a portal to a world of secret rituals, profound symbolism, and a unique worldview that captivated minds and hearts for centuries. This book aims to unravel this mysterious cult, exploring its origins, beliefs, rituals, and the complex historical setting in which it emerged and thrived.

To understand Mithraism, it is crucial to situate it in the context of the vast and multifaceted Roman Empire. This empire, which at its peak stretched across three continents, was a melting pot of cultures, ethnicities, and, crucially, religions. Roman expansion, driven by the most efficient military machine of the time, not only conquered territories but also absorbed and integrated the beliefs and practices of the subjugated peoples. The result was an unprecedented religious syncretism, where traditional Roman gods coexisted with Greek, Egyptian, Eastern, and Celtic deities, in a complex and constantly evolving mosaic.

In this environment of religious effervescence, the search for more personal and initiatory spiritual experiences gained strength. Traditional civic religions, focused on public worship and the maintenance of social order, began to lose their appeal for those seeking a more intimate connection with the divine, an answer to profound existential questions, and a sense of individual purpose. It was in this context that the so-called "Mystery Religions" thrived, offering secret rituals, promises of salvation, and a path of initiation that culminated in a transformative experience, often promising immortality or a more auspicious afterlife.

Mithraism fits perfectly into this category. Emerging sometime during the 1st century AD, possibly with roots in older Persian traditions, it quickly spread throughout the Roman Empire, from the farthest frontiers to the heart of the capital. Its popularity was particularly notable among the Roman military, which earned it the nickname "Religion of the Soldiers," but its appeal extended to various social strata, including merchants, civil servants, and even slaves.

What made Mithraism so attractive? Part of the answer lies in its mysterious and initiatory character. Unlike public religions, Mithraism was a mystery cult, meaning that its rituals and teachings were kept secret, revealed only to initiates. Admission to the cult was not automatic, but rather a gradual process of initiation, involving rites of passage, oaths of secrecy, and progression through seven hierarchical grades. This initiatory structure conferred a sense of exclusivity and belonging to the members, creating a strong group identity and fueling the curiosity of those outside.

Mithraic places of worship, known as mithraea (singular mithraeum), were invariably built as artificial caves or adapted from existing underground spaces. This architectural choice was not arbitrary, but deeply symbolic, referring to the legend of Mithras' birth from a rock and evoking the atmosphere of mystery and secrecy that permeated the cult. Inside the mithraea, initiates gathered to participate in elaborate rituals, including ritual meals, sacred banquets, and initiatory ceremonies that sought to recreate the myths and deeds of Mithras.

At the center of Mithraic belief was the myth of the Tauroctony, the iconic representation of Mithras slaying a sacred bull. This image, ubiquitous in Mithraic art, was not merely a narrative scene, but rather a complex and multifaceted symbol that encapsulated the cosmology, theology, and soteriology of the cult. The death of the bull, far from being an act of gratuitous violence, was interpreted as an act of cosmic creation, a primordial sacrifice that gave rise to the universe and allowed the renewal of life. Around this central myth, a rich tapestry of other stories and auxiliary deities developed, forming a complex and coherent religious system.

In addition to deep symbolism and mysterious rituals, Mithraism offered its adherents a clear ethical and moral structure, based on virtues such as loyalty, discipline, camaraderie, and self-control. These virtues, particularly valued in the military context, resonated with Roman ideals of masculinity and civic duty, but also offered a path of personal improvement and the pursuit of spiritual "light." Mithraism was not just a set of rituals and beliefs, but also a way of life, a practical philosophy that shaped the conduct and worldview of its initiates.

A crucial aspect of Mithraism is its relationship with Christianity, the religion that would eventually become dominant in the Roman Empire and, subsequently, in the Western world. Mithraism and Christianity emerged and expanded in the same historical period, competing for the same religious "market," so to speak. Both cults offered messages of salvation, initiatory rituals, a sense of community, and a moral structure. Although there are superficial similarities between the two, such as the practice of ritual meals and the belief in a savior deity, the theological and practical differences were profound, reflecting fundamentally different worldviews. The competition between Mithraism and Christianity, and the factors that led to the eventual triumph of the latter, are crucial themes for understanding the religious dynamics of the late Roman Empire and the legacy of Mithraism.

Throughout this book, we will delve deeply into the world of Mithraism, exploring every facet of this fascinating and mysterious cult. From its obscure origins and its expansion throughout the Roman Empire, to its secret rituals performed in dark caves, the enigmatic symbolism of the bull, and its complex relationship with Christianity, we will unravel the mysteries of Mithraism, seeking to understand what made it so attractive to its adherents and what its legacy is for the history of religion and spirituality. For the modern reader, in search of spiritual alternatives and contact with ancestral wisdom, Mithraism offers a window into a lost world of mystery and meaning, an invitation to explore an alternative spiritual path that, although long forgotten, still resonates with the human search for transcendence and meaning in life.

Chapter 2
The Setting of the Roman Empire

To truly understand the rise and popularity of Mithraism, it is not enough to simply analyze the intrinsic characteristics of the cult itself. It is essential to delve into the complex and multifaceted setting of the Roman Empire, the historical and cultural terrain where this religion flourished. The Roman Empire, at its zenith, was not only a formidable political and military entity, but also a vibrant center of cultural, social, and, crucially, religious exchange. This melting pot of influences, marked by diversity, syncretism, crises of values, and unprecedented expansion, created an exceptionally fertile environment for the emergence and proliferation of new religions, among which Mithraism stood out.

The Roman Empire, from its earliest days, demonstrated a remarkable capacity to absorb and integrate foreign cultures and religions. As Rome expanded, conquering territories and subjugating diverse peoples, it did not rigidly impose its own religion, but rather intelligently incorporated the deities and religious practices of the conquered peoples into its own pantheon. This phenomenon, known as religious syncretism, was a hallmark of Roman religiosity. Local gods were often identified with Roman deities, reinterpreted and integrated into the official cult of the Roman state. This process not only facilitated the assimilation of conquered peoples, but also enriched the Roman pantheon itself, making it increasingly eclectic and comprehensive.

However, religious syncretism in the Roman Empire was not limited to the incorporation of foreign gods into the traditional Roman pantheon. It went much further, creating an environment where different religious traditions coexisted and influenced each other. Temples dedicated to Egyptian, Greek, Oriental, and Celtic deities could be found in various parts of the empire, often side by side with temples dedicated to traditional Roman gods. This religious diversity was not seen as a problem, but rather as an inherent characteristic of the cosmopolitan nature of the empire. The Roman authorities generally adopted a tolerant attitude towards different cults, as long as they did not threaten public order and loyalty to the emperor.

This tolerance and openness to religious diversity created an environment where new religions could emerge and spread with relative ease. The Roman Empire was traversed by busy trade routes, by military legions in constant movement, and by a continuous flow of people of different origins and cultures. This intense cultural and human exchange facilitated the dissemination of religious ideas, ritual practices, and new forms of spirituality. Religions that emerged in one corner of the empire could quickly spread to other regions, finding fertile ground in an environment already accustomed to religious diversity.

However, the religious landscape of the Roman Empire was not only marked by diversity and syncretism, but also by a gradual crisis of traditional religious values. The archaic Roman religion, with its civic rituals and focus on maintaining the pax deorum (peace with the gods), was beginning to lose some of its appeal, especially for those seeking a more personal and emotional religious experience. The military conquests and territorial expansion, which had initially been seen as a sign of divine favor, also brought with them new social and existential problems.

Growing urbanization, increasing social complexity, and economic inequalities generated a sense of alienation and insecurity in many. Traditional civic religions, with their focus on the collective and the well-being of the state, seemed to offer few answers to individual anxieties and yearnings. The search for a sense of personal purpose, for a more intimate connection with the divine, and for promises of individual salvation intensified. This spiritual vacuum opened space for the flourishing of new forms of religiosity that offered precisely what traditional religions seemed to no longer provide: a more personal, emotional, and initiatory religious experience.

In this context, the so-called "Mystery Religions" gained prominence. These cults, often originating in the East, such as the Eleusinian Mysteries in Greece or the Egyptian cults of Isis and Osiris, offered secret rituals, promises of initiation, and a path to individual salvation.

Unlike public religions, which focused on collective rites and the maintenance of cosmic order, mystery religions emphasized individual experience, personal transformation, and the search for a mystical union with the deity. The secret and initiatory character of these cults, far from driving people away, attracted them, conferring a sense of exclusivity and access to esoteric knowledge reserved only for initiates.

Mithraism, as already mentioned, fits perfectly into this category of mystery religions. It shared with other mystery cults the emphasis on secret rituals, the initiatory structure with hierarchical degrees, and the promise of salvation. However, Mithraism also possessed distinctive characteristics that made it particularly attractive in the context of the Roman Empire. Its focus on the figure of Mithras, a warrior god and savior, resonated with the military values and martial culture of Roman society, especially among the soldiers of the Roman army. The masculine and fraternal atmosphere of the mithraea, the places of Mithraic worship, created a strong sense of camaraderie and belonging, aspects particularly important for men who spent long periods away from home, serving on the frontiers of the empire.

Furthermore, the rich and complex symbolism of Mithraism, with its elaborate cosmology, the myth of the Tauroctony, and enigmatic iconography, offered a sophisticated and intellectually stimulating belief system that could attract those seeking a deeper understanding of the universe and their place in it. The promise of salvation and a more auspicious afterlife, implicit in

Mithraic rituals and myths, was also a factor of great appeal in a world marked by uncertainty and mortality.

In short, the Roman Empire of the 1st century AD and onwards offered an exceptionally conducive setting for the emergence and expansion of new religions, such as Mithraism. Religious diversity, syncretism, the crisis of traditional values, and the search for more personal and meaningful spiritual experiences created fertile ground for mystery cults that offered secret rituals, promises of salvation, and a sense of community. Mithraism, with its distinctive characteristics and multifaceted appeal, knew how to take advantage of this environment, becoming one of the most popular and influential religions of the Roman Empire, competing directly with nascent Christianity and leaving a lasting legacy in the history of religion.

Chapter 3
The Origins of Mithras

One of the most fascinating and, at the same time, most enigmatic aspects of Mithraism lies in its origins. Unlike religions such as Christianity, which have a relatively well-documented historical founder and a set of canonical scriptures, the origins of Mithraism are shrouded in mystery, academic debate, and a notable scarcity of direct textual sources. Although archaeology has revealed much about the practice and iconography of the cult, the precise origins of Mithras and his cult remain a complex puzzle, challenging historians and scholars of religion for centuries.

The central question that permeates the debate about the origins of Mithras is: where did this god and this cult that spread so rapidly throughout the Roman Empire come from? The answer is not simple and is far from consensual. The evidence points to a complex interplay of influences, dating back to ancient Persian religious traditions, possibly with even more remote echoes in Indo-Iranian deities. However, how these influences were transmitted, adapted, and transformed in the Roman context to give rise to the Mithraism we know is a process still largely obscure and the subject of various interpretations.

One of the most important clues to understanding the origins of Mithras lies in the very name of the deity. "Mithras" is not a Roman name, but rather a name of Persian and Indo-Aryan origin. In ancient Persia, there was a divinity called Mithra, venerated in Zoroastrianism, the predominant religion of the Persian Empire. Likewise, in the Vedic traditions of India, we find a deity named Mitra, associated with the sun, pacts, and friendship. This onomastic connection strongly suggests that Roman Mithraism must have some connection, direct or indirect, with these Eastern religious traditions.

However, the precise nature of this connection is at the heart of the debate. One of the most traditional theories, once widely accepted, proposed that Roman Mithraism was a direct derivation of Persian Zoroastrianism, brought to the West by magian priests or through cultural contacts between the Roman Empire and the Persian Empire. According to this view, Roman Mithraism would essentially be a "Romanized" form of Zoroastrianism, adapted to the cultural and religious context of the Roman Empire.

This theory, however, has been increasingly questioned and criticized by modern scholars. Although the etymological connection of the name Mithras and the existence of deities with similar names in Persian and Vedic traditions is undeniable, the evidence for a direct transmission of Zoroastrianism to Roman Mithraism is scarce and problematic. The ritual practices, iconography, and theology of Roman Mithraism, as we know them through archaeology and scarce textual sources, show significant differences from Zoroastrianism. The Tauroctony, the central myth of Mithraism, for example, has no direct parallel in Zoroastrianism, and the auxiliary deities of the Mithraic pantheon are largely different from Zoroastrian deities.

A more nuanced perspective, currently more accepted by scholars, suggests that Roman Mithraism was not a direct derivation of Zoroastrianism, but rather a new religious creation that emerged in the context of the Roman Empire, but which drew inspiration from various religious traditions, including, but not limited to, Persian and Indo-Iranian traditions. In this view, the name "Mithras" and some general ideas about a deity associated with the sun and pacts could have been "borrowed" from Eastern traditions, but were reinterpreted and radically transformed in the Roman context, giving rise to a new and distinct cult.

This process of reinterpretation and adaptation would be facilitated by the environment of religious syncretism in the Roman Empire, already discussed in previous pages. In the Roman cultural melting pot, religious ideas and motifs traveled freely, being constantly reinterpreted and recombined. The name of an Eastern deity could be adopted, but filled with new meanings, rituals, and myths, adapted to the sensibilities and spiritual needs of the Roman public.

In this context, some scholars suggest that Roman Mithraism could have arisen in border regions of the Roman Empire, where contact with Eastern cultures was more intense, such as in Asia Minor or Syria. These regions were true centers of cultural exchange, where

Eastern and Western religious traditions met and mingled. Roman soldiers, merchants, and other travelers who circulated through these regions could have come into contact with Eastern religious ideas and practices, including the name and some vague notions about a god named Mithras. Upon returning to other parts of the empire, these individuals could have begun to develop and propagate a new cult, based on these Eastern impressions, but shaped and adapted to the Roman context.

It is important to note that Roman Mithraism itself seems to have presented itself from the beginning as an "Eastern" religion, exotic and mysterious. The mithraea, the places of worship, were often decorated with iconography that evoked the East, such as Persian clothing and representations of exotic landscapes. This aura of mystery and exoticism could have been part of the cult's appeal, attracting those seeking an alternative to traditional Roman religions, perceived by some as overly formal and devoid of mystery.

In short, the origins of Mithras and Roman Mithraism remain shrouded in mystery and debate. Although the etymological connection with Persian and Vedic deities is undeniable, the precise nature of this connection and the process of formation of Roman Mithraism are still the subject of speculation and research. The most accepted view today is that Roman Mithraism was not a simple derivation of Zoroastrianism, but rather a new religious creation that emerged in the context of the Roman Empire, inspired by various traditions, including Persian ones, but radically transformed and adapted to the Roman cultural and religious environment.

This mysterious and debated character of the origins of Mithraism does not diminish its fascination, but, on the contrary, increases it. The mystery surrounding the origins of Mithras contributes to the enigmatic aura of the cult, inviting us to delve deeper into its history, iconography, and symbolism, seeking to unravel the secrets of a religion that, although long gone, continues to intrigue and arouse the curiosity of the modern reader.

Chapter 4
From the Frontiers to the Heart of the Empire

After investigating the mysterious and debated origins of Mithraism, the next logical step in our journey is to trace its impressive geographical expansion throughout the vast Roman Empire. Mithraism, which emerged sometime in the 1st century AD, did not remain confined to a specific region or a small group of followers. On the contrary, it spread with remarkable speed and efficiency, leaving archaeological traces from the remotest frontiers of the empire, such as Britannia and Dacia, to the pulsating heart of the capital, Rome, and its most central provinces. Understanding how and why Mithraism was able to expand so comprehensively is crucial to appreciating its importance and influence in the Roman world.

The expansion of Mithraism did not occur in a vacuum, but rather in close connection with the social, political, military, and commercial dynamics of the Roman Empire. The Roman military machine, the backbone of the empire and the main engine of its territorial expansion, played a key role in the dissemination of the Mithraic cult. As already mentioned, Mithraism became particularly popular among Roman soldiers, especially in the legions stationed on the frontiers of the empire. The Roman legions were not only military forces, but also important centers of cultural exchange and dissemination of ideas. As the legions moved, built camps and settled in new regions, they carried with them not only Roman culture, but also their religious beliefs, including Mithraism.

Roman soldiers, when transferred from one region to another or when retiring and settling in different parts of the empire, disseminated the Mithraic cult wherever they went. Roman military camps, castra, often became centers of Mithraic worship, with the construction of mithraea within or near military bases. These mithraea served as places of worship for the soldiers, but could also attract members of the local civilian population, especially those who had contact with the military, such as merchants, artisans, and family members. In this way, Roman military bases acted as true poles of irradiation of Mithraism, driving its expansion to remote and frontier regions of the empire.

In addition to military expansion, Roman trade routes also played a crucial role in the spread of Mithraism. The Roman Empire was crisscrossed by an extensive network of roads, sea and river routes that facilitated trade and the movement of people and goods. Merchants, sailors, and other travelers who traveled these routes disseminated not only products, but also ideas and religious beliefs. Mithraism, with its appeal to diverse social strata, including merchants and artisans, found in trade routes an effective means of spreading.

Commercial ports, market towns, and urban centers along Roman trade routes became important centers for the diffusion of Mithraism. In busy port cities such as Ostia (port of Rome), Carthage, Alexandria, and Antioch, mithraea have been discovered, indicating the presence and popularity of the cult among merchant and urban communities. These urban centers acted as connecting nodes in trade networks, radiating Mithraism to neighboring regions and into the interior of the empire.

The dissemination of Roman culture, which accompanied military and commercial expansion, also contributed to the success of Mithraism. The Latin language, Roman culture, and the empire's infrastructure facilitated communication and the exchange of religious ideas. Mithraism, although with possibly Eastern origins, adapted and integrated into Roman culture, using the Latin language in its rituals and iconography, and adopting certain aspects of Roman culture. This "romanization" of Mithraism may have facilitated its acceptance and spread among the Roman population and in the western provinces of the empire.

Archaeological evidence is fundamental to confirm the wide expansion of Mithraism throughout the Roman Empire. The discovery of hundreds of mithraea in various regions of the empire, from Britain and Germany in the north, to Numidia and Egypt in the south, and from the Iberian Peninsula in the west, to Syria and Mesopotamia in the east, attests to the geographical scope of the cult. These mithraea, with their distinctive architectural and decorative features, provide a map of the expansion of Mithraism, revealing the paths the cult traveled and the centers where it established itself most strongly.

The concentration of mithraea in frontier and military regions, such as along the Danube, Rhine and Roman Limes (fortified border), reinforces the link between Mithraism and the Roman army. Cities such as Carnuntum (in present-day Austria), Dura-Europos (in Syria) and Vindobona (Vienna) have revealed significant mithraea complexes associated with Roman military bases. Similarly, the presence of mithraea in major urban and port centers, such as Rome, Ostia, Trier and London, demonstrates the popularity of the cult in urban and commercial contexts.

The distribution of mithraea is not uniform, however. Significant concentrations are found in the western provinces of the empire, such as Italy, Gaul, Germany and Britain, while the presence of the cult appears to have been less intense in the eastern provinces, such as Greece, Egypt and Asia Minor, paradoxically the regions closest to the possible eastern origins of Mithraism. This geographical distribution suggests that Mithraism, although with possibly Eastern roots, became more popular and widespread in the Roman West, adapting better to the cultural and religious context of the western provinces.

Analysis of the iconography and artifacts found in mithraea also contributes to understanding the expansion of Mithraism. The standardization of Mithraic iconography, especially the image of the Tauroctony, in mithraea across the empire suggests a relative cohesion and unity of the cult, despite its wide geographical dispersion. Ritual objects, such as chalices, torches, knives and representations of Mithraic deities, found in mithraea in different regions, demonstrate the similarity of ritual practices and fundamental beliefs of Mithraism throughout the empire.

In summary, the expansion of Mithraism throughout the Roman Empire was a remarkable phenomenon, driven by the complex interplay of military, commercial and cultural factors. The Roman legions, trade routes and the spread of Roman culture acted as vectors for the spread of the cult, taking it from the remotest frontiers to the heart of the empire. Archaeological evidence, represented by the vast distribution of mithraea throughout the Roman world, confirms the geographical scope of Mithraism and its importance as one of the most popular and influential religions of the Roman Empire.

Chapter 5
Mithras and the Roman Army

One of the most distinctive and often cited aspects of Mithraism is its deep and lasting connection to the Roman army. From the remotest frontiers of the empire to the heart of Rome, archaeological traces of Mithraism reveal an overwhelming presence in military contexts. Mithraea, the places of Mithraic worship, have been discovered in large numbers within Roman military bases (castra), in border fortresses, in legionary camps and in naval ports, indicating that the cult of Mithras became, in many ways, an "army" religion within the Roman Empire. This strong connection between Mithraism and the army is not merely a demographic coincidence, but rather a reflection of the intrinsic characteristics of the cult that resonated particularly well with the values, needs, and life experiences of Roman soldiers.

To understand the appeal of Mithraism to the Roman military, it is essential to consider the context of Roman military life and the values that were cultivated within the legions. The life of a Roman soldier was rigorous, demanding, and often dangerous. Soldiers spent long periods away from home, on duty on the frontiers of the empire, facing adverse weather conditions, constant dangers, and the ever-present threat of armed conflict. Discipline, loyalty, courage, physical and mental endurance, and camaraderie were essential virtues for survival and military success. Mithraism, with its structure, symbolism, and value system, offered a belief system that harmonized remarkably well with this military ethos.

One of the main attractions of Mithraism for soldiers was its emphasis on camaraderie and fraternity. The mithraea were closed and communal ritual spaces where initiates gathered to participate in secret rituals, ritual meals, and sacred banquets. These ritual practices fostered a strong sense of unity and solidarity among members of the Mithraic community, echoing the camaraderie that was vital to the cohesion and effectiveness of Roman military units. For soldiers living far from their families and civilian communities, the mithraeum offered a space of belonging, a "home away from home," where they could find mutual support, companionship, and a sense of collective identity.

The initiatory structure of Mithraism, with its seven hierarchical degrees, could also resonate with the military mindset, accustomed to hierarchies, promotions, and a system of progression. The journey through the Mithraic degrees, from Corax to Pater, could be seen as a metaphor for progression in a military career, with each degree representing a new level of knowledge, responsibility and status within the Mithraic community. Discipline and obedience, fundamental military values, were also emphasized in the Mithraic context, with initiates being subjected to oaths of secrecy and a strict code of conduct.

Mithraic virtues, such as courage, loyalty, discipline, and self-control, were also military virtues par excellence. The myth of Mithras as a warrior god, who fought against the forces of darkness and triumphed over chaos, could inspire Roman soldiers, offering a divine model of heroism and resilience. Mithraic iconography, often decorating military mithraea, reinforced these messages, presenting Mithras as a victorious warrior, a protector and a spiritual guide for his followers.

The promise of a more auspicious afterlife, implicit in Mithraic rites and myths, could also be particularly appealing to soldiers, who faced death more imminently and frequently than the civilian population. Belief in the immortality of the soul or in a post-mortem journey guided by Mithras could offer comfort and hope in the face of the mortality inherent in military life. For a Roman soldier, the idea that Mithraic initiation could ensure safe passage to the other world or union with Mithras himself could be a powerful incentive to join the cult.

The archaeological evidence of the link between Mithraism and the Roman army is overwhelming. Mithraea have been discovered in numerous Roman castra along borders such as the Danube, Rhine, Euphrates and Hadrian's Wall in Britain. In some cases, mithraea were built within the walls of military bases, demonstrating the integration of worship into the daily lives of soldiers. In other cases, mithraea were found near military camps, serving as places of worship for soldiers and other individuals associated with military bases.

The mithraeum of Dura-Europos, a Roman frontier town on the Euphrates, is a notable example of the link between Mithraism and the army. This mithraeum, located within the city walls and possibly frequented by Roman soldiers stationed there, is one of the best preserved and most richly decorated that we know of. The murals of the Dura-Europos mithraeum offer a fascinating glimpse into Mithraic iconography and the cult's ritual practices in a military context.

In Rome, the presence of mithraea on the Caelian Hill, a region traditionally associated with military barracks, and the discovery of mithraea under imperial buildings, such as the Baths of Caracalla, suggest that the cult also found adherents among members of the Praetorian Guard and other military units stationed in the capital. The city of Ostia itself, the port of Rome and base of the Classis Misenensis (Roman fleet of Misenum), revealed a remarkable concentration of mithraea, reflecting the popularity of Mithraism among Roman sailors and naval personnel.

Mithraic iconography also reflects its connection to the military world. Representations of Mars, the Roman god of war, and Victoria, the personification of victory, are found in some mithraea, indicating an association between Mithraism and Roman military ideals. Some Mithraic initiates are depicted wearing military uniforms or carrying weapons, suggesting that military identity was an important part of Mithraic identity for some adherents. The figure of Mithras himself, often depicted as a vigorous young warrior, may have been seen as a role model by Roman soldiers.

It is important to note, however, that Mithraism was not exclusively a military cult. Although its connection with the Roman army is undeniable and strongly documented, archaeological and epigraphic evidence shows that the cult also attracted members of other social strata, such as merchants, public officials, freedmen, and even slaves. However, the predominance of mithraea in military contexts and the nature of Mithraic values and symbolism confirm that the Roman army was one of the main vectors of dissemination and one of the social groups most receptive to Mithraism.

In conclusion, the strong link between Mithraism and the Roman army is one of the most striking and defining characteristics of this mysterious cult. Mithraism offered Roman soldiers a belief system that resonated with their values, needs, and life experiences, providing camaraderie, discipline, a clear moral code, a model of divine heroism, and the promise of a more auspicious afterlife. The Roman legions, as they moved throughout the empire, acted as important disseminators of Mithraism, taking the cult from the remotest frontiers to the heart of the Roman world, making it truly "the cult of the soldiers."

Chapter 6
The Social Diversity of Mithraism

Although the connection between Mithraism and the Roman army is undeniable and constitutes one of the most prominent characteristics of the cult, reducing Mithraism to a mere "soldiers' religion" would be an oversimplification and inaccurate. Archaeological and epigraphic evidence, while confirming the strong military presence in Mithraism, also reveals that the cult attracted followers from a surprising variety of social strata within the Roman Empire. Merchants, civil servants, freedmen, slaves, and even members of the Roman aristocracy, in smaller numbers, left traces of their adherence to Mithraism, demonstrating that the cult's appeal transcended the boundaries of military camps and extended to different segments of Roman society.

To understand the social diversity of Mithraism, it is crucial to recognize that the Roman Empire was a complex and stratified society, with a wide range of professions, social classes, and legal statuses. Roman society was not monolithic, but rather a mosaic of social groups with different interests, needs, and aspirations. Mithraism, with its flexibility and adaptability, managed to offer something of value to different segments of this diverse society, finding resonance in different social groups beyond the military.

A notable social group, besides soldiers, that adhered to Mithraism in significant numbers was that of merchants. The Roman trade routes, as we have seen in previous pages, played a fundamental role in the expansion of Mithraism, and urban and port centers along these routes became important centers of Mithraic worship. Merchants, sailors, and other professionals linked to commerce formed a mobile and cosmopolitan social group, who traveled extensively throughout the empire and came into contact with different cultures and religions. Mithraism, with its aura of oriental mystery and its message of protection and good fortune, may have attracted merchants who sought security and prosperity in their travels and business.

The discovery of mithraea in important commercial centers, such as Ostia, the port of Rome, and in merchant cities along the Rhine and Danube, reinforces the connection of Mithraism with merchant communities. Dedicatory inscriptions in mithraea often mention dedicants who identify themselves as *negotiatores* (merchants) or *mercatores* (merchants), confirming the presence and importance of this social group in the Mithraic cult. For merchants, who often lived in cosmopolitan and mixed communities, Mithraism may have offered a sense of community and identity beyond ethnic and regional boundaries, uniting them around a common cult and shared values.

Another social group that found appeal in Mithraism was that of civil servants and imperial administrators. The Roman Empire depended on a vast bureaucracy to govern its vast territories and manage its complex administrative systems. Civil servants, from the lowest ranks to the highest positions in the imperial administration, played a crucial role in maintaining order and the functioning of the empire. These individuals, often educated and with a certain level of social mobility, could be attracted to Mithraism for various reasons.

Mithraism, with its hierarchical structure and elaborate rituals, could appeal to the sense of order and organization that was valued in Roman administration. Mithraic virtues, such as discipline, loyalty, and duty, also resonated with the ideals of public service and administrative responsibility. In addition, Mithraism, as a mystery religion, could offer a space for initiation and esoteric knowledge for intellectually curious individuals seeking something beyond traditional civic religion.

Inscriptions in mithraea mention dedicants identified as *officiales* (officials) and other administrative positions, indicating the presence of civil servants in the Mithraic cult. For these individuals, Mithraism could represent a more personal and engaging form of religiosity than formal civic rites, offering a deeper spiritual experience and a sense of belonging to a select community.

Surprisingly, Mithraism also attracted members of the lower social strata of Roman society, including freedmen and slaves. Although slavery was a fundamental institution in Roman society, slaves were not completely excluded from religious life. Some mystery cults, such as Mithraism, seem to have offered a space for social inclusion and hope for marginalized and underprivileged individuals.

The discovery of mithraea in humble urban contexts and the mention of dedicants with names of servile origin suggest that slaves and freedmen participated in Mithraism. For these individuals, who lived in precarious living conditions and with few opportunities for social advancement, Mithraism could offer a promise of spiritual equality and redemption beyond earthly social hierarchies. The Mithraic brotherhood, the community experience of rituals, and the promise of individual salvation could be particularly attractive to those who felt excluded and marginalized by Roman society.

It is important to note that the adherence of slaves to Mithraism challenges the notion that the cult was exclusively a "soldiers' religion" or of social elites. The presence of slaves in mithraea demonstrates the ability of Mithraism to transcend social barriers and offer a universal appeal, encompassing different strata of Roman society. For slaves, Mithraism could represent a space of spiritual freedom and human dignity, where they could find a sense of belonging and value beyond their social condition.

Even members of the Roman aristocracy, although in smaller numbers compared to the military and other social groups, also left traces of their adherence to Mithraism. Dedicatory inscriptions of individuals with noble names and the discovery of mithraea on rural properties of aristocratic families suggest that the cult also found adherents among the Roman elites. For these individuals, who already enjoyed social privileges and political power, the appeal of Mithraism could lie in other factors, such as the search for a more exclusive and initiatory religious experience, the fascination with Eastern mystery, or the attraction to a form of religiosity. more personal and emotional than traditional civic religion.

In summary, the social diversity of Mithraism is a crucial aspect to understanding its success and widespread dissemination in the Roman Empire. Although the connection with the Roman army is undeniable, Mithraism was not an exclusively military cult, but rather a religion that managed to attract followers from different social strata, including merchants, civil servants, freedmen, slaves, and even members of the aristocracy. The appeal of Mithraism for these diverse social groups lay in its ability to offer answers to different spiritual, social, and existential needs. For the military, it offered camaraderie, discipline, and a moral code; for merchants, security and prosperity; for civil servants, order and a familiar hierarchical system; for slaves and freedmen, hope and social inclusion; and for elites, mystery and a more exclusive religious experience.

The social diversity of Mithraism demonstrates the complexity and adaptability of this mysterious cult, which managed to flourish in the cultural and social melting pot of the Roman Empire, offering an alternative spiritual path and a sense of community to a wide range of individuals.

Chapter 7
The Tauroctony and the Birth of Mithras

At the heart of Mithraism, pulsating as the life force that animates the entire system of beliefs and rituals, lies the myth of the Tauroctony. This iconic scene, omnipresent in Mithraic art and repeatedly represented in sculptures, reliefs, and paintings in mithraea throughout the Roman Empire, is not merely one narrative among many, but rather the central myth, the sacred story that summarizes the cosmology, theology, and soteriology of the cult. The Tauroctony, the representation of Mithras killing a sacred bull, is the defining image of Mithraism, a complex and multifaceted symbol that radiates meaning in multiple directions, unraveling the mysteries of creation, sacrifice, and cosmic renewal. To truly understand Mithraism, we must first delve into the depths of the myth of the Tauroctony and unlock its secrets.

The scene of the Tauroctony is, at first glance, enigmatic and even disturbing. At the center of the representation, we find Mithras, typically portrayed as a vigorous young man, wearing a Phrygian cap (a characteristic cap associated with the region of Phrygia, in Asia Minor, and also a symbol of freedom in the Roman context) and a flowing cloak. He is kneeling on an immense bull, subduing it with strength and determination. With his left hand, Mithras pulls the bull's head back, while with his right hand he plunges a knife or sword into the animal's neck. The bull, subdued but still powerful, struggles in agony, with blood gushing from the wound.

However, the scene of the Tauroctony is not only composed of Mithras and the bull. A series of other figures and symbolic elements populate the representation, enriching it with additional layers of meaning. A dog and a snake leap towards the bull's wound, licking the gushing blood. A scorpion grabs the bull's testicles with its pincers. A raven hovers nearby, sometimes perched on Mithras' cloak or elsewhere in the scene. Ears of wheat sprout from the bull's tail or from the blood that flows from the wound. The Sun and the Moon, often represented as anthropomorphic deities, observe the scene from above, each on one side of the representation.

In addition to these central figures, we often find the representations of Cautes and Cautopates, two young men dressed similarly to Mithras, but on a smaller scale, who flank the scene of the Tauroctony. Cautes, to the right of Mithras, holds a raised torch, pointing upwards, symbolizing dawn and growth. Cautopates, to the left of Mithras, holds an inverted torch, pointing downwards, symbolizing dusk and decline. These two dadophoroi (torchbearers) represent cosmic opposites, the daily cycle of the sun and the dynamic balance of the universe.

The interpretation of the Tauroctony has been the subject of intense debate among scholars of Mithraism. However, a general consensus has emerged around the idea that the scene represents a myth of cosmic creation and renewal of life. The death of the bull, far from being an act of destructive violence, is understood as a primordial sacrifice, a necessary act to give rise to the cosmos and allow the continuity of life. From the bull's blood, its spinal cord and its semen, vital elements for the world are born: plants, animals and human life itself. The wheat that sprouts from the bull's tail symbolizes the fertility and abundance that emanate from the primordial sacrifice.

In this interpretation, Mithras is not seen as a mere bull slayer, but rather as a cosmic creator, an agent of primordial sacrifice that makes the existence of the ordered universe possible. The bull, in turn, represents the primordial life force, the raw and chaotic energy that needs to be subdued and sacrificed in order for order and life to emerge. The sacrifice of the bull is, therefore, a founding act, a cosmic event that marks the beginning of creation and establishes order in the universe.

The animals that accompany the Tauroctony also play important symbolic roles. The dog, the snake and the scorpion, by feeding on the sacrificed bull, represent the forces of nature that benefit from the primordial sacrifice, ensuring the continuity of the cycle of life. The raven, messenger of the Sun, may be associated with communication between the divine world and the earthly world, or with other aspects of the myth that still escape us. The Sun and the Moon, celestial witnesses of the Tauroctony, represent the cosmic order and universal harmony that result from the sacrifice. Cautes and Cautopates, with their ascending and descending torches, personify the cycle of time and the fundamental duality of existence.

The Tauroctony, therefore, is not just an isolated scene, but rather the center of a complex mythical and symbolic system. It is closely linked to other myths and stories about Mithras, including his miraculous birth from a rock. According to legend, Mithras was not born in the traditional way, but rather emerged as an adult from a rock petrogenetrix (generating stone), holding a knife and a torch. This stony birth, represented in some Mithraic scenes, emphasizes the divine and extraordinary nature of Mithras, separating him from the natural order and associating him with a primordial and mysterious origin.

The myth of Mithras' birth from the rock complements the myth of the Tauroctony, offering a more complete view of the figure of Mithras and his role in the cosmos. If the Tauroctony presents him as the cosmic creator through sacrifice, the birth of the rock establishes him as a primary divinity, emerging from the very substrate of reality, predestined to carry out his cosmic feats. The knife and torch that Mithras wields at birth already foreshadow his role as agent of sacrifice and bearer of light, central elements of his divine mission.

Together, the myths of the Tauroctony and the birth of Mithras form the core of the Mithraic mythical narrative, offering an overview of the cult's cosmology, theology and soteriology. Mithras emerges as a primordial divinity, born from the rock and destined to perform the cosmic sacrifice that gives rise to the universe and allows the renewal of life. The Tauroctony, the central myth of Mithraism, encapsulates this founding narrative, presenting itself as a powerful and enigmatic symbol that invites contemplation and interpretation on multiple levels.

Chapter 8
The Life Cycle of Mithras

Although the Tauroctony takes center stage in Mithraic iconography and theology, representing the foundational myth of primordial sacrifice and cosmic creation, the life cycle of Mithras is not limited to this single monumental event. Around the Tauroctony, a rich tapestry of other myths and stories is woven, complementing the central narrative and expanding our understanding of the figure of Mithras, his divine deeds, and the Mithraic belief system as a whole. These secondary narratives, although less ubiquitous in Mithraic art than the Tauroctony, are crucial for understanding the depth and complexity of Mithraic mythology, revealing other facets of Mithras' character and enriching the religious experience of initiates.

One of the most important myths that complements the Tauroctony is the aforementioned birth of Mithras from the rock. This myth, known as petrogenesis (birth from stone), narrates the miraculous birth of Mithras not from a human mother, but directly from a petra genetrix, a primordial rock. Artistic representations of this myth, although less frequent than those of the Tauroctony, show Mithras emerging as an adult from the rock, often naked, but always carrying his distinctive attributes: the curved knife (or sword) and the Phrygian cap. Sometimes torches are also depicted beside the rock, prefiguring Mithras' role as the bearer of light.

The myth of the rock birth emphasizes the extraordinary and divine nature of Mithras, separating him from the natural and human order. His birth is not earthly, but cosmic, emerging from a primordial element of creation. The rock, as a symbol of solidity, eternity, and origin, reinforces the idea of Mithras as a primary deity, pre-existing the created world itself. The knife and the torch, which Mithras already wields at birth, foreshadow his destiny and his mission: the knife, as the instrument of sacrifice in the Tauroctony, and the torch, as a symbol of the light that he will bring to the world. This miraculous birth establishes Mithras as an exceptional being, destined to perform great deeds and play a central role in Mithraic cosmology.

Other stories and legends about Mithras narrate his miraculous deeds and his prowess. Although there is no Mithraic textual canon that relates these stories systematically, we infer their existence from scattered references in texts by Christian authors who polemicized against Mithraism, and from artistic representations that illustrate episodes from Mithras' life beyond the Tauroctony. Among these feats, the legend of Mithras making water spring from a rock with an arrow stands out. This narrative echoes the myth of the rock birth, reinforcing Mithras' connection with rocks and his ability to extract life and sustenance from the inanimate element.

Other legends may have narrated Mithras' hunting skills, depicting him as a vigorous and fearless hero, dominating wild animals and demonstrating his strength and dexterity. Hunting, as an activity associated with nobility and bravery in the Roman world, could reinforce the image of Mithras as a model of martial virtue, especially for his military followers. Some artistic representations show Mithras engaged in hunting scenes, confirming the existence of these narratives.

A myth of particular importance is that of the pact or alliance between Mithras and the Sun (Sol Invictus). According to this narrative, Mithras and the Sun initially clashed in combat, but after a vigorous duel, they recognized each other's strength and entered into a pact of friendship and collaboration. This pact is often represented artistically as a handshake scene between Mithras and the Sun, sealing the alliance. In some more elaborate representations, this pact is followed by a sacred banquet, where Mithras and the Sun share a meal, sealing their union and establishing a harmonious cosmic order.

The myth of the pact between Mithras and the Sun is of great theological and cosmological importance in Mithraism. The Sun, as the source of light and life, occupies a central place in Mithraic cosmology, being often associated with the supreme divinity itself, or at least with a superior manifestation of divine power. The alliance between Mithras and the Sun represents the union of two fundamental cosmic forces, establishing a dynamic and harmonious balance in the universe. The sacred banquet that follows the pact symbolizes the communion and cooperation between these cosmic forces, ensuring the order and prosperity of the world.

This myth also explains the hierarchical relationship between Mithras and the Sun in the Mithraic pantheon. Although Mithras is the central hero of the cult and the agent of the primordial sacrifice, the Sun is often revered as a superior deity, or at least as a more direct manifestation of supreme divine power. The Mithraic degree of Heliodromus ("Sun-Runner"), the fifth in the initiatory hierarchy, suggests the importance of the Sun in the Mithraic system, and the very designation of Sol Invictus (Unconquered Sun), often associated with Mithraism, reinforces this solar centrality.

The life cycle of Mithras culminates with his ascension to heaven. After completing his earthly mission and establishing cosmic order through the Tauroctony and the pact with the Sun, Mithras ascends to the celestial realm, joining the Sun and the other gods. This ascension is often represented artistically as Mithras being raised to heaven in a chariot, driven by the Sun itself, or by other divine beings. In some representations, the sacred banquet between Mithras and the Sun precedes the ascension, marking the climax of Mithras' earthly journey and his definitive entry into the divine realm.

The myth of Mithras' ascension to heaven is fundamental to Mithraic soteriology, that is, to the understanding of salvation and the final destiny of the soul in Mithraism. The ascension of Mithras serves as a model and a promise for Mithraic initiates. Just as

Mithras ascended to heaven after completing his earthly journey, initiates hoped, through initiation and the practice of Mithraic rituals, to follow Mithras' path and achieve immortality or a blessed existence after death. The Mithraic degree of Pater ("Father"), the highest in the initiatory hierarchy, may be associated with this promise of ascension and the emulation of Mithras' divine destiny.

Together, these myths and stories, in addition to the Tauroctony, compose a rich and multifaceted life cycle of Mithras. From his miraculous birth from the rock, through his heroic deeds, the pact with the Sun, and culminating in his ascension to heaven, Mithraic mythology offers a panorama of Mithras' divine journey, his role as creator and orderer of the cosmos, and his final destiny as a celestial deity. These narratives, although fragmentary and dispersed, contribute to the construction of a complex and fascinating image of Mithras, the central hero of the mystery cult that captivated so many followers in the Roman Empire.

Chapter 9
The Universe in Seven Spheres

Beyond the myths and rituals that we explored previously, Mithraism possessed an elaborate and sophisticated cosmology, which provided a map of the universe and humanity's place within it. This cosmology, although not fully explained in direct Mithraic texts (given the secretive nature of the cult), can be reconstructed from archaeological and iconographic evidence and references in ancient authors. At the center of this Mithraic worldview lies the concept of the universe structured in seven planetary spheres, a common cosmological idea in the ancient world, but one that in Mithraism acquired a particular meaning and a deep integration with the cult's soteriology and ritual practice.

The idea of the seven planetary spheres was not an original invention of Mithraism. On the contrary, it was a cosmological model widely disseminated in the Greco-Roman world and the Near East, with roots in Babylonian astronomy and astrology and Greek philosophy, particularly in the Platonic and Stoic traditions. This cosmological model postulated that the universe was organized in a series of concentric spheres, each corresponding to one of the seven celestial bodies visible to the naked eye that moved differently from the "fixed stars": the Moon, Mercury, Venus, the Sun, Mars, Jupiter and Saturn, in ascending order of distance from Earth (in the geocentric view prevalent in antiquity).

In the Mithraic context, these seven planetary spheres were not just astronomical entities, but also cosmic realms with spiritual and symbolic meaning. Each sphere was associated with a specific planet, and by extension, with the astrological and mythological characteristics attributed to that planet in ancient astrology. The order of the spheres, from closest to Earth to farthest, reflected not only their physical position in the cosmos, but also a spiritual hierarchy and a path of ascension for the soul.

The seven planetary spheres in Mithraism were generally associated with the following planets and characteristics:

Moon (First Sphere): The sphere closest to Earth, associated with the feminine principle, generation, growth, change, the sublunar world, and the first stages of the soul's journey.

Mercury (Second Sphere): Associated with communication, intelligence, commerce, eloquence, cunning, and transition between worlds, serving as a guide for the soul.

Venus (Third Sphere): Associated with love, beauty, harmony, pleasure, passion, fertility, and the reconciliation of opposites, representing a stage of emotional purification for the soul.

Sun (Fourth Sphere): The central point, the sphere of the Sun, associated with light, life, reason, order, justice, the supreme divinity (Sol Invictus), and the point of balance and illumination in the soul's journey.

Mars (Fifth Sphere): Associated with war, courage, strength, aggression, action, discipline, and overcoming obstacles, representing a test of the moral and spiritual strength of the soul.

Jupiter (Sixth Sphere): Associated with royalty, wisdom, law, cosmic order, divine justice, prosperity, and reward, representing a stage of wisdom and spiritual authority for the soul.

Saturn (Seventh Sphere): The farthest sphere, associated with time, fate, melancholy, introspection, death, transcendence of earthly limits, and the threshold of the fixed star realm, representing the final stage of the soul's journey before union with the divine.

This cosmological model of the seven planetary spheres was not just a static description of the universe, but a dynamic map of the soul's journey after death. In the Mithraic context, it was believed that the human soul, after the death of the physical body, began a journey of ascension through these seven planetary spheres, towards the realm of the fixed stars and, ultimately, union with the divine. This journey of the soul through the spheres was seen as a process of purification, spiritual ascension, and progression through different levels of cosmic existence.

Each planetary sphere represented a stage of purification and transformation for the soul. By ascending through each sphere, the soul was to free itself from the earthly impurities and passions associated with the ruling planet of that sphere, acquiring the corresponding virtues and spiritual qualities. For example, when passing through the sphere of Venus, the soul would purify its earthly desires and passions, learning love and harmony; when ascending through the sphere of Mars, it would overcome its aggression and impulsiveness, cultivating courage and discipline; and so on, until reaching the sphere of Saturn, where it would completely free itself from the bonds of the material world and prepare for the final ascension.

Mithraic iconography often reflects this cosmology of the seven spheres. Some mithraea were decorated with representations of the seven planets and the signs of the zodiac, suggesting that the ritual space was seen as a microcosm, a reflection of the universe ordered in spheres. The seven degrees of Mithraic initiation may also be related to the seven planetary spheres, with each degree representing a stage of the spiritual journey and a progressive approach to divinity. The very structure of the mithraeum, often built as a dark and vaulted cave, may have been designed to evoke the cosmos and the soul's journey through the spheres.

The cosmology of the seven spheres also implied an astrological view of the universe in Mithraism. It was believed that the planets, in their orbits through the spheres, exerted influence on the sublunar world and on human life. Astrology, widely practiced in the Roman world, was probably integrated into the Mithraic belief system, with initiates seeking to understand planetary influences and align themselves with cosmic forces to facilitate their spiritual journey. The choice of names for the Mithraic degrees (Corax, Nymphus, Miles, Leo,

Perses, Heliodromus, Pater) may also reflect astrological and planetary associations, although precise interpretations vary among scholars.

In short, the Mithraic cosmology of the seven planetary spheres represents a fundamental element for understanding the cult's worldview. This cosmological model was not just a description of the physical universe, but a spiritual map of the soul's journey, a path of purification, ascension, and union with the divine. The cosmology of the seven spheres was deeply integrated with Mithraism's soteriology, ritual practice, and symbolism, providing a frame of reference for the initiates' religious experience and their search for transcendence and meaning in life.

Chapter 10
The Mithraic Pantheon

Although Mithras occupies the central and indisputable position in the Mithraic cult, being the mythical hero, the agent of the Tauroctony, and the soteriological guide of the initiates, the Mithraic pantheon is not limited to this singular figure. Around Mithras gravitate a series of auxiliary deities and symbolic figures that enrich the religious system, complementing its theology and cosmology. These entities, although less prominent than Mithras in artistic representations and existing literature, play important roles in the mythical narrative, rituals, and Mithraic worldview, revealing the complexity and richness of the Mithraic pantheon beyond the central figure of the bull-slaying god.

Among the auxiliary deities most frequently represented and mentioned in Mithraic contexts, Cautes and Cautopates stand out, the dadophoroi or torchbearers who flank the scene of the Tauroctony. These two young figures, dressed similarly to Mithras, but on a smaller scale, are almost omnipresent in the representations of the Tauroctony, and also appear in separate scenes, often associated with the Sun and the Moon. Cautes and Cautopates personify the cosmic duality of light and darkness, day and night, dawn and dusk, representing the complementary opposites that structure the universe and the cycle of time.

Cautes, generally positioned to the right of Mithras in the Tauroctony (from the observer's point of view), holds a raised and ascending torch. This gesture symbolizes the dawn, the rising sun, the light that emerges from the darkness, growth, life ascending, and the creative and ascending force of the cosmos. Cautes is often associated with spring, east, and the ascending celestial hemisphere. His name may be related to the Persian word for "conscience" or "vigilance", suggesting a connection with enlightenment and spiritual awakening.

Cautopates, in turn, positioned to the left of Mithras, holds an inverted and descending torch. This gesture symbolizes dusk, the setting sun, the light that declines into darkness, decline, death (in the sense of transformation and not annihilation), and the descending and transforming force of the cosmos. Cautopates is often associated with autumn, west, and the descending celestial hemisphere. His name may derive from a combination of Persian words meaning "he who guards" or "he who protects", suggesting a function as guardian of the threshold between day and night, life and death.

Cautes and Cautopates, in their complementary duality, represent the fundamental dualistic principle of Mithraic cosmology, the constant and balanced struggle between light and darkness, good and evil, creation and destruction, life and death. This duality is not seen as an irreconcilable conflict, but rather as an essential dynamic for the existence of the ordered universe. The interaction and complementarity between Cautes and Cautopates ensure the cycle of time, the alternation between day and night, the seasons, and ultimately the continuity of life.

Another auxiliary deity of importance in the Mithraic pantheon is Sol Invictus, the Unconquered Sun. Already mentioned in the context of the myth of the pact between Mithras and the Sun, Sol Invictus occupies a prominent position in the Mithraic divine hierarchy, often being revered as the supreme deity or as a superior manifestation of divine power. The cult of Sol Invictus already existed in the Roman world before the emergence of Mithraism, but it was integrated and reinterpreted in the Mithraic context, becoming a central piece of the cult's theology.

In Mithraism, Sol Invictus is often represented as a radiant and powerful deity, associated with light, life, cosmic order, divine justice, and celestial royalty. He is seen as the primordial source of all light and life in the universe, and as the supreme ruler of the cosmos. The pact between Mithras and Sol Invictus establishes a relationship of collaboration and harmony between the two deities, with Mithras acting as the agent of Sol Invictus in the sublunar world, performing the sacrifice of the Tauroctony and guiding the souls of the initiates on their spiritual journey.

Although the precise hierarchical relationship between Mithras and Sol Invictus is a subject of debate, the evidence suggests that Sol Invictus was generally considered superior to Mithras in the Mithraic pantheon.

The degree of initiation of Heliodromus ("Runner of the Sun"), the fifth in the Mithraic hierarchy, indicates a special veneration of the Sun, and the very designation of "Sol Invictus" emphasizes his invincibility and supremacy. In some representations, Sol Invictus is shown crowning Mithras or granting him power, symbolizing his superior authority.

In addition to Cautes, Cautopates, and Sol Invictus, other deities and symbolic figures populate the Mithraic pantheon, although with less frequency and prominence. The Moon, as the celestial counterpart of the Sun, is also often represented in Mithraic scenes, especially associated with Cautopates, reinforcing the light-darkness and Sun-Moon duality. The Ocean (Oceanus), the primordial deity of the waters that surround the world, sometimes appears in Mithraic representations, symbolizing the primordial forces of nature and the aquatic substratum of creation.

Other symbolic figures, such as the seasons, the winds, and the cosmic elements, can be inferred from some representations and descriptions, although they are not personified as distinct deities. The signs of the zodiac, as already mentioned in the context of Mithraic cosmology, also play an important symbolic role, representing the celestial influences and the cosmic order that govern the universe and human life.

It is important to note that the Mithraic pantheon was not a rigid and dogmatic system, but rather a flexible and adaptable set of deities and symbols, which could vary in detail and emphasis between different mithraea and regions of the Roman Empire. Mithraism, as a mystery religion, allowed a certain latitude in the interpretation and expression of beliefs, as long as the central figures and fundamental principles of the cult were maintained.

In summary, the Mithraic pantheon, although centered on the figure of Mithras, is not limited to this singular deity. Cautes and Cautopates, Sol Invictus, the Moon, and other symbolic figures enrich the religious system, representing cosmic principles, forces of nature, and aspects of divinity that complement the central figure of Mithras. This complex and multifaceted pantheon reflects the sophistication of Mithraic theology and its ability to integrate various religious and philosophical influences from the Greco-Roman and Eastern world.

Chapter 11
Fundamental Principles and Beliefs

After exploring the Mithraic pantheon and the auxiliary deities that compose it, it is crucial to turn our focus to the core of Mithraic theology, that is, the system of fundamental beliefs and principles that sustained this mysterious cult. Although Mithraism does not possess a set of canonical scriptures or formal doctrinal statements, we can reconstruct its theological principles from the analysis of myths, rituals, iconography, and the scarce indirect textual references. In doing so, a picture emerges of a sophisticated and coherent theology, centered around ideas such as cosmic dualism, the quest for salvation, the immortality of the soul, and a rigorous ethical code.

One of the most prominent and defining theological principles of Mithraism is cosmic dualism. As we have already alluded to when discussing Cautes and Cautopates, Mithraism perceived the universe as a cosmic battlefield, a stage for the incessant struggle between opposing forces, personified by the duality between light and darkness, good and evil. This dualistic vision of the cosmos was not exclusive to Mithraism, being a recurring theme in various religions and philosophies of the ancient world, especially in the

Persian and Iranian traditions, which possibly influenced Mithraism.

In the Mithraic context, this cosmic dualism manifested itself in multiple forms. The aforementioned opposition between Cautes and Cautopates, bearers of the ascending and descending torch, personified the duality between day and night, dawn and dusk, light and darkness. The myth of the Tauroctony itself, with the struggle between Mithras and the primordial bull, can be interpreted as a representation of the struggle between order and chaos, creation and destruction, good and evil. Mithraic iconography often used symbols of light and darkness, such as the Sun and the Moon, or light and dark colors, to emphasize this fundamental duality.

This cosmic dualism was not just a metaphysical description of the universe, but also an existential and moral reality for Mithraic initiates. It was believed that the struggle between good and evil was reflected in the human world and in the very soul of each individual. Human life was seen as a microcosmic battlefield, where the forces of light and darkness fought for dominance over the soul. The Mithraic initiate was called to take sides in this cosmic struggle, aligning himself with the forces of light and fighting the darkness within himself and in the outside world.

Salvation occupies a central place in Mithraic theology, although the precise nature of Mithraic salvation is still a subject of debate and interpretation. Unlike some religions that promise salvation as a free divine gift, Mithraism seems to emphasize the necessity of human effort, initiation, and ritual practice to achieve salvation. Initiation into the Mithraic mysteries, with progression through the seven grades, was seen as a path of spiritual ascent and purification of the soul, preparing the initiate for the post-mortem journey and for union with the divine.

The figure of Mithras plays a crucial role in Mithraic soteriology. As the agent of the Tauroctony, Mithras is the cosmic savior who overcomes primordial chaos and establishes order in the universe. He is also the guide and protector of the initiates, leading them on the spiritual journey and offering them the promise of salvation. The imitation of Mithras, through participation in Mithraic rituals and the adoption of Mithraic virtues, was seen as a path to individual salvation.

The immortality of the soul is another fundamental belief of Mithraic theology, although the precise nature of the afterlife in Mithraism is unclear due to the scarcity of direct sources. The ascension of Mithras to heaven, after completing his earthly mission, served as a model and a promise for the initiates. It was believed that, through initiation and ritual practice, the soul of the initiate could follow the path of Mithras and ascend to the celestial realm after the death of the physical body.

The cosmology of the seven planetary spheres, discussed earlier, is closely linked to Mithraic soteriology and the belief in the immortality of the soul. The journey of the soul through the spheres, after death, was seen as a process of purification and spiritual ascension, culminating in union with the divine in the realm of the fixed stars or beyond. Mithraic rituals, performed in the mithraea that represented microcosms of the ordered universe, aimed to prepare the soul for this post-mortem journey, strengthening and purifying it for ascension through the spheres.

Mithraic theology also included an ethical and moral code that guided the conduct of initiates. This ethical code, although not explicitly formulated in Mithraic texts, can be inferred from iconography, rituals, and references in ancient authors. Mithraic virtues, such as loyalty, discipline, courage, camaraderie, honesty, self-control, and resilience, were highly valued and promoted within the cult.

These virtues, as already mentioned in the context of Mithraism's connection with the Roman army, resonated with military ideals and traditional Roman values. However, in the Mithraic context, these virtues acquired a deeper spiritual and religious dimension. They were not just desirable qualities for earthly life, but also essential requirements for the spiritual journey and for the fight against the forces of darkness, both internal and external. The Mithraic initiate was called to live according to these ethical principles, seeking moral and spiritual perfection as part of his path to salvation.

The search for light is a recurring theme in Mithraic theology and symbolism. Light, as opposed to darkness, is a central symbol of good, truth, knowledge, order, and divinity. Mithras is often associated with light, being represented as a torchbearer and as an emissary of Sol Invictus, the primordial source of all light. Mithraic initiation, with its rituals performed in dark and subterranean mithraea, can be interpreted as a symbolic journey from darkness to light, a process of spiritual enlightenment and awakening to divine truth.

The metaphor of light and darkness permeates Mithraic theology, representing the cosmic struggle between good and evil, but also the path of the soul in search of enlightenment and salvation. The Mithraic initiate was called to follow the path of light, to reject the darkness of error, ignorance, and evil, and to seek union with the primordial source of divine light.

In summary, Mithraic theology, although fragmentary and reconstructed from various indirect sources, reveals a coherent and sophisticated belief system, centered around principles such as cosmic dualism, the quest for salvation, the immortality of the soul, and a rigorous ethical code. Mithras, as the central figure of this system, is the cosmic savior, the spiritual guide, and the model of virtue for the initiates. Mithraic theology offered its adherents a comprehensive worldview and a well-defined spiritual path, responding to their existential needs and offering a sense of purpose and hope in a complex and uncertain world.

Chapter 12
The Path of the Initiate

Having explored the intricate Mithraic theology and the pantheon of divinities that orbit Mithras, it becomes imperative to investigate how these transcendental principles translated into a practical ethical and moral system for the initiates. Mithraism was not merely a set of abstract beliefs or esoteric rituals; it offered a concrete way of life, a code of conduct that shaped the behavior and choices of its followers in their daily lives. Ethics and morality in Mithraism were not mere adornments, but rather the very foundation upon which the "path of the initiate" was built, the journey of spiritual improvement and search for light that characterized the Mithraic religious experience.

As we have already outlined in previous pages, Mithraic cosmology was intrinsically dualistic, perceiving the universe as a battlefield between the forces of light and darkness, good and evil. This cosmic duality echoed on the plane of human existence, where each individual found themselves immersed in this incessant struggle. Mithraic ethics and morality thus emerged as essential tools for the initiate to align themselves with the forces of light, combat inner and outer darkness, and tread the path of salvation and spiritual ascension. The "path of the initiate" was, in essence, a path of moral improvement, a continuous effort to embody Mithraic virtues and live in harmony with the cosmic order.

At the heart of Mithraic ethics, we find a set of fundamental virtues, moral qualities that guided the conduct of initiates and defined the ideal of Mithraic perfection. Although there is no formal catechism listing these virtues, we can infer them from Mithraic iconography, ritual practices, and indirect references in ancient texts. Among the most prominent Mithraic virtues, the following stand out:

Loyalty (Fidelity): Loyalty was a primordial virtue in Mithraism, manifesting itself on several levels. Loyalty to Mithras, the divine hero and savior; loyalty to the Mithraic community, the brotherhood of initiates; and loyalty to oaths of secrecy and ritual commitments. Loyalty was the cement that united the Mithraic community, creating bonds of solidarity and mutual trust, essential for a mystery cult that depended on discretion and secrecy. For soldiers, loyalty was a fundamental military value, and its transposition to the religious sphere in Mithraism reinforced the cult's appeal to this social group.

Discipline (Self-control): Discipline, both physical and mental, was highly valued in Mithraism. Self-control, the ability to master impulses and passions, was seen as essential for spiritual progress and for life in harmony with the cosmic order. Discipline manifested itself in strict adherence to rituals, fulfillment of oaths, moderation in pleasures, and the constant pursuit of self-improvement. For the military, discipline was an inherent virtue of military life, and Mithraism internalized and spiritualized this value, transforming it into a pillar of religious ethics.

Courage (Valor): Courage, bravery in the face of danger and challenges, was another prominent Mithraic virtue. The life of the initiate, like that of the soldier, was seen as an arduous journey, full of trials and obstacles. Courage was needed to face these challenges, both on the material and spiritual planes. Mithraic courage was not only physical bravery on the battlefield, but also the moral courage to maintain faith, persevere on the path of initiation, and combat the forces of inner and outer darkness.

Comradeship (Brotherhood): Comradeship, the spirit of unity and mutual support among the members of the Mithraic community, was a fundamental value. The mithraea were spaces for fraternal encounter and fellowship, where initiates supported each other on their spiritual journey. Ritual meals and sacred banquets promoted social cohesion and a sense of belonging to the Mithraic brotherhood. Comradeship was especially important for soldiers, who found in Mithraism an extension of military camaraderie, a fraternal bond that transcended ties of blood and social origin.

Honesty (Integrity): Honesty, truthfulness, and moral rectitude were virtues expected of Mithraic initiates. Moral integrity, the coherence between principles and conduct, was seen as essential for spiritual progress and for maintaining order within the Mithraic community. Honesty manifested itself in truthfulness in oaths, righteousness in business dealings, and sincerity in interpersonal relationships within the brotherhood.

Self-control (Temperance): Self-control, moderation in desires and passions, was a valued virtue in Mithraism, in line with Stoic philosophy and other currents of thought of the time. Mastery over impulses and appetites was seen as essential for the purification of the soul and liberation from the shackles of the material world. Self-control manifested itself in moderation in food and drink, control of sexuality, and restraint of negative emotions such as anger and envy.

Resilience (Perseverance): Resilience, the ability to endure difficulties and persevere in the face of adversity, was an essential virtue for the Mithraic initiate. The path of initiation was long and arduous, requiring continuous effort and unwavering dedication. Resilience was necessary to overcome obstacles on the spiritual path, to maintain faith in times of trial, and to persevere in the pursuit of light, even in the face of darkness.

These Mithraic virtues were not just abstract ideals, but guiding principles for the daily conduct of initiates. Mithraic ethics manifested themselves in the way initiates related to each other within the community, how they behaved towards non-initiates, and how they conducted their lives in general. Loyalty to the Mithraic community translated into active participation in rituals, mutual support among members, and discretion regarding the secrets of the cult. Discipline was reflected in the observance of ritual rules, moderation in pleasures, and the pursuit of constant self-improvement. Courage was manifested in the firmness of faith, perseverance in trials, and defense of Mithraic values.

The Mithraic moral code was intrinsically linked to ritual practice. Initiation rituals, sacred banquets, prayers, and Mithraic hymns were not just formal ceremonies, but also transformative experiences that aimed to shape the moral and spiritual character of the initiates. The oaths of secrecy, uttered during initiations, were not just commitments to discretion, but also declarations of moral intent, reinforcing the importance of honesty and fidelity to Mithraic principles. Ritual meals, shared in community, promoted camaraderie and fraternity, encouraging the practice of the virtue of solidarity.

The "path of the initiate" in Mithraism was, therefore, a continuous moral and spiritual journey. Progression through the seven initiatory degrees was not just a hierarchical ascent, but also a process of ethical refinement and spiritual growth. Each Mithraic degree could be associated with specific virtues to be cultivated and moral challenges to be overcome. The ultimate goal of this path was the complete transformation of the initiate, their progressive approximation to the ideal of moral and spiritual perfection represented by Mithras, and their eventual ascension to the realm of light.

In contrast to other moral systems of the time, such as Roman civic ethics or the emerging Christian ethics, Mithraic morality was characterized by its initiatory and internal character. It was not so much a code of public conduct or external laws, but rather a set of internalized moral principles, to be cultivated within the individual through initiation and religious practice. Mithraic ethics was a morality of personal improvement, aimed at the inner transformation of the initiate and their individual spiritual journey.

In conclusion, ethics and morality in Mithraism were essential and intrinsic elements of the cult. The Mithraic virtues, such as loyalty, discipline, courage, comradeship, honesty, self-control, and resilience, formed the moral code that guided the conduct of initiates and defined the "path of the initiate." This path was a continuous journey of moral and spiritual improvement, driven by ritual practice and the pursuit of light, aiming at the inner transformation of the initiate and their eventual salvation. Mithraic ethics was not just a set of rules, but a practical philosophy of life, a guide for daily conduct and a roadmap for the spiritual journey, shaping the identity and religious experience of the followers of the cult of Mithras in the Roman Empire.

Chapter 13
The Sacred Cave and the Ritual Space

Beyond the complex myths, dualistic theology, and rigorous ethics, the religious experience of Mithraism was profoundly shaped by the mithraeum, the distinctive and essential place of worship for initiates. The mithraeum, invariably conceived as a sacred cave, artificially constructed or adapted from natural underground spaces, was not merely a functional building for performing rituals. On the contrary, it was a ritual space charged with symbolism, carefully designed and decorated to evoke a mysterious and transcendental atmosphere, transporting initiates to a microcosm that reflected the cosmic order and facilitated their spiritual journey. Understanding the mithraeum as a sacred and ritual space is fundamental to unraveling the secrets of Mithraic religious practice and the mystical experience it provided to its adherents.

The choice of the cave as an architectural model for the mithraeum was not arbitrary, but deeply symbolic and loaded with meaning within the Mithraic context. The cave, as a dark, subterranean, and mysterious natural formation, possessed a rich symbolic charge in various ancient cultures, often associated with the underworld, chthonic forces, the mystery of life and death, and rebirth. In Mithraism, the cave referred directly to the myth of the birth of Mithras from the rock (petrogenesis), a founding event that established the divine and extraordinary origin of the central hero of the cult. The mithraeum, by replicating the cave environment, invoked this primordial myth, symbolically recreating the birthplace of Mithras and transforming it into a sacred space, imbued with the divine presence.

The architecture of the mithraeum generally followed a relatively consistent pattern, although with regional variations and adaptations to available spaces. The mithraeum was typically a narrow, elongated, and underground or semi-subterranean space, designed to evoke the dark and claustrophobic atmosphere of a natural cave. Natural light was intentionally limited, or even completely absent, creating an environment of twilight and mystery, conducive to introspection and mystical experience. Access to the mithraeum was often through a narrow and discreet entrance, reinforcing the idea of a secret space reserved only for initiates.

The interior space of the mithraeum was generally divided into three main zones:

The antechamber (or vestibule): An entrance space, often less elaborate than the main body of the mithraeum, serving as a preparation and transition area for initiates before entering the ritual space itself.

The central corridor (or nave): The main space of the mithraeum, elongated and narrow, with benches (podia) arranged along the side walls. These benches, usually raised and built of masonry or wood, were intended to accommodate initiates during Mithraic rituals and banquets. The central corridor was the main location for the performance of the cult's rituals and ceremonies.

The sanctuary (or apse): Located at the opposite end of the mithraeum entrance, the sanctuary was the focal point of the ritual space, where the central representation of the Tauroctony was located. The image of the Tauroctony, sculpted in relief, painted, or sculpted in the round, was placed in a niche, on an altar, or simply against the wall of the apse, visually dominating the mithraeum and serving as the central object of veneration and contemplation.

The decoration of the mithraeum was carefully crafted and rich in Mithraic symbolism. In addition to the ubiquitous representation of the Tauroctony in the sanctuary, the walls, ceiling, and floor of the mithraeum were often decorated with paintings, reliefs, and sculptures that illustrated other Mithraic myths, represented auxiliary divinities (such as Cautes and Cautopates, Sol Invictus, etc.), zodiacal, planetary, and cosmic symbols. Mithraic decoration was not merely ornamental, but an integral part of the ritual space, reinforcing the mysterious atmosphere and conveying theological and cosmological messages to initiates.

The colors used in the decoration of the mithraea were often symbolic. Blue, gold, and red, for example, were recurring colors, associated with the sky, the sun, and the blood of life, respectively. The use of blue on the vaulted ceiling of some mithraea aimed to evoke the night sky and the celestial sphere, reinforcing the idea of the mithraeum as a microcosm of the universe. Gold could be used to represent the sun and divine light, while red could symbolize the blood of the Tauroctony sacrifice and the vital force emanating from it.

Artificial lighting in the mithraeum, from torches, oil lamps, or candles, played a crucial role in creating the mysterious and ritualistic atmosphere. The flickering and dim light, casting dancing shadows on the decorated walls, intensified the cavernous character of the space and contributed to the sensory and emotional experience of the initiates. Light, in Mithraism, was a central symbol of good, truth, and divinity, and artificial lighting in the mithraeum symbolically evoked the search for spiritual light and the overcoming of the darkness of ignorance and evil.

The mithraeum, as a ritual space, was the place where the rituals and ceremonies of the Mithraic cult unfolded, from initiations into the different hierarchical degrees to sacred banquets and ritual meals. The mithraeum was, therefore, a stage for the enactment of the Mithraic mysteries, a space of ritual performance where myths came to life and initiates actively participated in the recreation of the sacred history of Mithras. The mysterious atmosphere, symbolic decoration, and cavernous architecture of the mithraeum contributed to the effectiveness of the rituals, intensifying the religious experience and facilitating the inner transformation of the initiates.

The mithraeum, in its totality, can be understood as a microcosm, a small-scale representation of the ordered universe, as it was conceived in Mithraic cosmology. The cavernous form, evoking the womb of the earth and the birthplace of Mithras, symbolized the primordial origin of the cosmos. The zodiacal and planetary decoration, often present in mithraea, represented the celestial order and the cosmic influences that govern the world. The central representation of the Tauroctony, in the sanctuary, evoked the primordial act of creation and sacrifice that gave rise to the ordered universe.

Upon entering the mithraeum and participating in the rituals, initiates were, therefore, symbolically immersed in the Mithraic cosmos, transported to a sacred space where they could experience the divine presence, connect with the founding myths of the cult, and experience their own spiritual journey as a micro-reproduction of the cosmic journey of Mithras. The mithraeum was not just a place of worship, but a portal to the divine world, a liminal space where the profane and the sacred met, and where spiritual transformation became possible.

In short, the mithraeum, as the sacred cave and central ritual space of Mithraism, was much more than a simple building. It was a complex architectural and symbolic space, carefully designed to evoke a mysterious and transcendental atmosphere, transport initiates to the mythical world of Mithras, and facilitate their spiritual journey. The cavernous architecture, symbolic decoration, artificial lighting, and organization of the interior space converged to create a microcosm of the Mithraic universe, a sacred space where rituals came to life and the religious experience reached its maximum intensity.

Chapter 14
Initiation and the Mithraic Grades

At the pulsating heart of Mithraism, beyond the subterranean mithraea and enigmatic myths, resided a complex and structured initiatory system that defined the religious experience of its followers: initiation and the Mithraic grades. Mithraism was, par excellence, a mystery religion, and initiation constituted the gateway to esoteric knowledge and full participation in the life of the Mithraic community. The journey through the seven hierarchical grades, from Corax to Pater, represented a gradual and progressive spiritual path, a symbolic ascent towards enlightenment and union with the divine. Understanding the system of initiation and the Mithraic grades is fundamental to unraveling the internal dynamics of the cult, the religious experience of its members, and the promise of transformation that it offered.

The initiatory nature of Mithraism is one of its most distinctive features, contrasting with Roman civic religions, which were public in character and open to all citizens. Access to the Mithraic mysteries was not automatic but rather conditioned on a process of ritual initiation, involving rites of passage, oaths of secrecy, and progression through different levels of knowledge and participation. This initiatory structure gave Mithraism an exclusive and selective character, attracting those who sought a deeper, more personal, and transformative religious experience, reserved only for a select group.

Secrecy was a central element of Mithraic initiation. The rituals, teachings, and mysteries of the cult were kept in strict secrecy, revealed only to initiates and zealously guarded from the uninitiated. The oaths of secrecy, uttered during initiation ceremonies, bound members to an obligation of absolute discretion, under penalty of severe divine and community sanctions. This secrecy, far from being a mere artifice to generate mystery, was seen as essential to preserve the purity and efficacy of the rites, as well as to protect the Mithraic community from hostile external gazes.

Initiation into the Mithraic mysteries was a gradual and hierarchical process, organized into seven distinct grades, each with a specific name, symbolism, and associated rites of passage. These grades, in ascending order, were: Corax (Raven), Nymphus (Nymph), Miles (Soldier), Leo (Lion), Perses (Persian), Heliodromus (Sun-Runner), and Pater (Father). Progression through the grades was not automatic, but rather dependent on the evaluation of superiors, length of service, and possibly tests and trials that the initiate had to overcome. The hierarchy of grades reflected a social and spiritual structure within the Mithraic community, with each grade conferring different levels of knowledge, responsibilities, and prestige.

Each Mithraic grade was associated with a set of specific symbols, attributes, and responsibilities, reflecting the stage of the initiate's spiritual journey and their role within the community. Although detailed information about the rituals and teachings of each grade is scarce due to the secrecy of the cult, we can infer some elements from iconography, indirect textual references, and comparisons with other mystery cults.

Corax (Raven): The first grade, associated with the planet Saturn and the god Mercury. The raven, as a messenger and intermediary between worlds, symbolized the initiate as a servant of the community, responsible for mundane and preparatory tasks. The raven was associated with the element of air. Initiates in this grade may have performed functions as messengers, ritual assistants, or caretakers of the mithraeum.

Nymphus (Nymph): The second grade, associated with the planet Venus and the goddess Luna. The nymph, a figure of nature and water, symbolized purification, nourishment, and fertility. The Nymphus was associated with the element of water. Initiates in this grade may have participated in water purification rites and ritual meals, playing a serving role in ceremonies.

Miles (Soldier): The third grade, associated with the planet Jupiter and the god Mars. The soldier, as a representative of strength, courage, and discipline, symbolized initiation into active spiritual life, combat against the forces of darkness, and commitment to Mithraic values. The Miles was associated with the element of earth. Initiation into this grade involved a rite of military "recruitment," with the marking of the initiate with a branding iron (cautery) on the forehead and the offer of a crown, which the initiate had to refuse, stating that Mithras was his only crown. The Miles was the soldier of Mithras, committed to spiritual struggle and the defense of the community.

Leo (Lion): The fourth grade, associated with the planet Mars and the god Sol. The lion, a solar animal and symbol of strength, power, and royalty, represented a higher level of initiation, associated with solar energy, sacred fire, and identification with divine force. The Leo was associated with the element of fire. Rituals involving fire and purification by fire may have characterized this grade. Leo initiates may have had a more active role in rituals and ceremonies, perhaps as readers of ritual texts or assistants to the Pater in certain rites.

Perses (Persian): The fifth grade, associated with the planet Moon and the goddess Persephone (or Cybele). The "Persian" evoked the eastern origins of the cult and the ancestral wisdom of Persian traditions. This grade may have been associated with knowledge of Mithraic myths and cosmology, understanding of the mysteries of the cult, and transmission of tradition. The Perses may have been associated with multiple elements. Perses initiates may have had a role as instructors and catechists, transmitting Mithraic teachings to the lower grades.

Heliodromus (Sun-Runner): The sixth grade, associated with the planet Venus and the god Sol. The "Sun-Runner" evoked the journey of the Sun through the sky, the daily cycle of light, and the intimate connection with the solar deity Sol Invictus. This grade represented an even higher level of solar initiation, perhaps associated with the mystical experience of union with the Sun and the contemplation of divine light. The Heliodromus may have been associated with the element of aether. Heliodromus initiates may have had higher liturgical functions, perhaps presiding over certain rites or acting as intermediaries between the community and the solar deity.

Pater (Father): The highest grade of the Mithraic hierarchy, associated with the planet Saturn and the god Saturn (or Jupiter-Saturn). The "Pater" was the leader of the local Mithraic community, the priest responsible for conducting rituals, initiating new members, and transmitting tradition. The Pater represented the highest spiritual authority within the mithraeum and was seen as the representative of Mithras in the earthly community. The Pater may have been associated with purple, the color of royalty and authority. The Pater was the guardian of the Mithraic mysteries, the spiritual guide of the community, and the guarantor of the continuity of the cult.

The journey through the Mithraic grades can be interpreted on multiple levels. On a symbolic and spiritual level, it represents a gradual progression towards enlightenment, purification of the soul, and union with the divine. Each grade represents a stage of spiritual development, with challenges to be overcome and virtues to be cultivated. On a social and community level, the hierarchy of grades reflected the internal organization of the Mithraic community, with different levels of responsibility and participation. On a cosmological level, the journey through the grades can be seen as a representation of the soul's ascent through the planetary spheres, towards the celestial realm.

Mithraic initiation, with its secret rites and hierarchical grades, offered its followers a solid religious structure and a well-defined spiritual path. The initiate's journey, from Corax to Pater, represented a path of personal transformation and the pursuit of transcendence, providing a sense of purpose, belonging, and hope in a complex and uncertain world.

Chapter 15
Secret Rituals

At the heart of Mithraism resided a core of ritual practices shrouded in secrecy and mystery, which constituted the essence of the religious experience for initiates. Mithraism, as a mystery religion, thrived precisely on the veil of the hidden, on the promise of esoteric knowledge reserved only for those who underwent initiation rites and swore to maintain silence. These secret rituals, performed in the dark and cavernous interior of the mithraea, were the pulsating heart of the cult, the stage where Mithraic myths came to life, where initiates connected with the divine, and where spiritual transformation became possible. Unraveling, even partially, the mysteries of these secret rituals is a complex challenge, given the intentionally secretive nature of the cult, but exploration of archaeological, iconographic, and indirect textual clues can shed some light on the ritual practices that shaped the Mithraic experience.

The secret nature of Mithraic rituals was a defining feature of the cult, shared with other mystery religions of the Greco-Roman world. Secrecy was not merely an accidental characteristic, but rather an intrinsic and functional element of the Mithraic religious experience. Secrecy served multiple purposes: to protect the cult from external persecution or profanation, to guarantee the exclusivity and value of esoteric knowledge, to intensify the mystical experience and sense of belonging among initiates, and to preserve the purity and efficacy of the rites. The oaths of secrecy, uttered during initiations, bound members to a strict law of silence, under penalty of divine and community punishments, which explains the notable scarcity of direct descriptions of Mithraic rituals in textual sources.

Despite the veil of secrecy, we can infer the existence of different types of rituals in Mithraism, based on archaeological evidence and sparse references. The most likely ritual categories include:

Initiation Rituals: These rituals constituted the core of the Mithraic initiatory system, marking the passage of candidates through the seven hierarchical grades. Initiation rites were complex rites of passage, involving a series of trials, oaths, symbols, and ritual actions intended to transform the initiate, integrate them into the Mithraic community, and confer upon them the knowledge and privileges associated with each grade. Initiations may have included purification rituals, such as ablutions with water or purification with fire, tests of courage and endurance, enactment of Mithraic myths (possibly dramatizations of the Tauroctony or the birth of Mithras), communion rituals (ritual meals), and the revelation of esoteric teachings and secret symbols. The oaths of secrecy, uttered at each initiation, sealed the initiate's commitment to the community and to the protection of the Mithraic mysteries. The passage through each grade may have been symbolically interpreted as a ritual death to the old state and a rebirth to a new level of spiritual and community existence.

Sacred Banquets (Ritual Meals): Ritual meals, or sacred banquets, were a central practice in Mithraism, held regularly in mithraea and iconographically represented in some scenes. These banquets were not mere profane meals but rather ritual acts of communion and fraternity, performed in a sacred context and with deep religious significance. Mithraic ritual meals may have involved the consumption of symbolic food and drink, possibly bread and wine (or water with honey, as some evidence suggests), shared communally among initiates. These banquets may have reinforced social bonds between members of the Mithraic community, promoted a sense of unity and fraternal solidarity, and established a symbolic communion with the deity, possibly with Mithras and/or Sol Invictus. The atmosphere of the sacred banquets may have been one of celebration, conviviality, and sharing, creating a sacred space for spiritual and social communion.

Other Possible Rituals: In addition to initiations and sacred banquets, it is likely that Mithraism included other types of rituals, although the evidence is even more fragmentary and speculative. There may have been daily or weekly rituals performed in mithraea, such as prayers, hymns, offerings, and purification rites, intended to keep the flame of Mithraic devotion alive, strengthen the connection with the deity, and renew commitment to the values of the cult. Rites of passage to mark important events in the lives of initiates, such as births, marriages, or funerals, are also possible, although evidence is scarce. The precise nature of these rituals and their frequency remain largely unknown due to the veil of secrecy surrounding Mithraism.

The ritual actions performed in mithraea were laden with religious symbolism, conveying theological, cosmological, and ethical messages to initiates through body language, gestures, and ritual objects. Among the most common ritual actions, we can mention:

Purification Rites: Water and fire were important ritual elements in Mithraism, often used in purification rites. Ablution with water, or passing through flames (or symbolic representations of fire), may have been performed to cleanse the initiate of spiritual impurities, prepare them for sacred rites, and symbolize the purification of the soul on the path of initiation. Water, as an element of cleansing and renewal, and fire, as an agent of transformation and purification, were powerful symbols of spiritual renewal in the Mithraic context.

Communion: Ritual meals were, in themselves, acts of communion, but the concept of communion may have extended to other ritual practices. The sharing of bread and wine (or water with honey) could symbolize communion with the deity, the incorporation of divine qualities, or mystical union with Mithras or Sol Invictus. Communion, in a broader sense, could refer to the sharing of religious experience and community identity among initiates, strengthening fraternal bonds and the sense of belonging to the group.

Ritual Dramas (Myth Enactments): Although the evidence is indirect and speculative, it is possible that

Mithraic rituals included ritual dramas or enactments of Mithraic myths, especially the myth of the Tauroctony and the birth of Mithras. The dramatization of myths may have intensified the religious experience of initiates, making myths more vivid and emotionally impactful, allowing participants to identify with mythical figures and symbolically experience the events of sacred history. These ritual dramas could involve theatrical performances, music, chants, and symbolic actions, creating an intense sensory and emotional experience.

Symbolic Actions and Ritual Objects: Mithraic rituals certainly involved a series of symbolic actions, such as gestures, postures, ritual movements, and the use of ritual objects laden with meaning. Torches, representing divine light and the path of enlightenment; knives or swords, evoking the sacrifice of the Tauroctony and the strength of Mithras; chalices and paterae (shallow cups), used in sacred banquets; and other ritual objects may have been used to confer symbolic and ritualistic meaning to the actions performed, enriching the religious experience and communicating theological and cosmological messages non-verbally.

The ultimate goal of the secret Mithraic rituals was to provide initiates with a transformative religious experience that connected them with the divine, integrated them into the Mithraic community, and led them on the path of salvation. The rituals aimed to awaken altered states of consciousness, induce a sense of divine presence, promote spiritual purification, reinforce Mithraic beliefs and values, strengthen community ties, and offer the promise of a more auspicious afterlife. The Mithraic ritual experience was, in essence, a journey of personal transformation and the pursuit of transcendence, carried out in the mysterious and sacred environment of the mithraeum.

It is essential to recognize the limitations of our knowledge about Mithraic secret rituals. Due to the intentionally secret nature of the cult and the scarcity of direct textual sources, the precise reconstruction of Mithraic rituals remains a considerable challenge. We rely heavily on archaeological evidence, such as the architecture and decoration of mithraea, the ritual objects found, and iconographic representations, and on indirect references in ancient authors, often hostile to Mithraism (such as Christian authors). The interpretation of this evidence is largely speculative and conjectural, and many questions about Mithraic rituals remain unanswered.

Despite the limitations, the exploration of Mithraic secret rituals offers a fascinating glimpse into the religious experience of followers of the cult of Mithras. The rituals, with their mysterious atmosphere, symbolic actions, and promise of transformation, constituted the heart of Mithraic practice, shaping the religious identity of initiates and offering them an alternative spiritual path in the Roman world.

Chapter 16
Communion and Fraternity

In the intricate labyrinth of secret rituals that comprised Mithraism, ritual meals and Mithraic banquets occupied a prominent place, transcending the mere function of physical sustenance to become sacred acts of communion and fraternity. These celebrations, held in the mysterious atmosphere of the mithraea, represented crucial moments in the life of the Mithraic community, strengthening social bonds between initiates and providing a tangible experience of belonging to a select group, united by common beliefs and practices. Beyond the social aspect, Mithraic ritual meals carried a profound religious symbolism, evoking sharing, abundance, and union with the divine, central elements in the theology and soteriology of the cult. Exploring the meaning of these banquets, the food and drinks consumed, and the atmosphere that surrounded them is essential to understanding the communal and experiential dimension of Mithraism.

Mithraic ritual meals, often referred to as sacred banquets, were not occasional or peripheral events, but rather regular and central practices in the life of the mithraea. The exact frequency of these banquets is uncertain, but archaeological evidence, namely the recurring presence of dining spaces and kitchen utensils in mithraea, suggests that they occurred with relative regularity, possibly at monthly intervals or on specific festive dates of the Mithraic calendar, if such a calendar existed in a formalized way. These ritual gatherings provided initiates with the opportunity to come together in a sacred context, sharing not only food but also their faith and Mithraic identity.

The cavernous environment of the mithraeum intensified the atmosphere of these sacred banquets. The flickering light of lamps and torches, casting shadows on the walls decorated with mythical scenes, created a space isolated from the outside world, immersed in mystery and reverence. The very act of sharing food in an underground space, perhaps echoing ancestral chthonic rites, conferred a primordial and transcendent dimension to the banquets, distancing them from the profane meals of everyday life. The mithraeum, transformed into a sacred refectory, became a privileged meeting place between initiates and, symbolically, with the Mithraic deities.

The primary meaning of Mithraic banquets was communion. The word "communion" here assumes multiple meanings. Firstly, communion with the community. Ritual meals brought together the members of the Mithraic brotherhood, strengthening fraternal bonds and the sense of belonging to a cohesive group united by common values and beliefs. The sharing of food, a fundamental act of human sociability, created and reinforced social bonds, consolidating the collective Mithraic identity. In these banquets, profane social distinctions were likely attenuated, if not suspended, in favor of equality before the mysteries of Mithras and fraternity among initiates. Soldiers, merchants, public officials - men of different origins and social strata - gathered on an equal footing in the mithraeum, united by faith and participation in the mysteries.

Secondly, communion with the divine. Although the precise nature of Mithraic theology in relation to the divinity at banquets is debated, it is plausible that these ritual meals were interpreted as a form of symbolic communion with Mithras and/or Sol Invictus. The sharing of sacred food, performed in a consecrated space and with specific ritual formulas (although unknown to us), could be seen as a participation in the divine essence, a symbolic approach to the celestial sphere. Some scholars suggest that the very food and drink consumed at the banquets could be seen as representations or symbolic manifestations of the divinity, conferring upon participants a share of divine power and blessing.

Fraternity, intrinsically linked to communion, was another central element of Mithraic banquets. Mithraism, especially in its military aspect, valued camaraderie, loyalty, and mutual support among its members. The sacred banquets offered a ritualized context for the expression and reinforcement of these fraternal values. The sharing of food, the conviviality in a sacred environment, and the joint participation in rites created a bond of brotherhood among the initiates, transcending profane family and social ties. This Mithraic fraternity, forged in the mysteries and shared rituals, could have been particularly meaningful for soldiers, who found in the mithraeum an extension of military camaraderie, a space for conviviality and mutual support in a religious environment.

As for the food and drinks consumed at Mithraic banquets, archaeological and iconographic evidence, although fragmentary, offers some clues. The most frequent iconographic representation of a Mithraic banquet shows Mithras and Sol Invictus reclining on a kline (banquet couch), sharing a meal. This scene, often associated with the myth of the pact between Mithras and the Sun, suggests a divine model for Mithraic banquets, with celestial deities presiding over the ritual and sharing a sacred meal.

The specific foods consumed at Mithraic banquets probably varied according to region, time of year, and resources available in each mithraeum. However, some constants seem to emerge from the archaeological and iconographic evidence. Bread was certainly a fundamental food, present in virtually all cultures of the Roman world and easily accessible. Fragments of bread have been found in some mithraea, and its symbolic importance as a staple food and as a representation of the body (in other religions of the time) make its presence at Mithraic banquets highly likely.

Wine was also a ritually significant drink in the Roman world, and its presence at Mithraic banquets is equally likely, although less directly attested by archaeology. Wine, associated with blood, joy, and euphoria, could have played a symbolic role in Mithraic banquets, perhaps representing the blood of the sacrificed bull or the joy of communion with the divine. In some iconographic representations of Mithraic banquets, what appears to be a chalice or cup is presented between Mithras and the Sun, suggesting the consumption of a ritual drink, which could be wine or some other fermented beverage.

In addition to bread and wine, other foods could have been consumed at Mithraic banquets, complementing the meal and enriching the sensory experience. Meat, although there is no direct evidence of the consumption of bull meat (which would be unlikely given the respect for the animal), could have been consumed in other forms, such as poultry or small animals, depending on availability and local practices. Fruits, vegetables, cheeses, and honey could also have been part of the Mithraic banquet menu, complementing the meal and offering a variety of flavors and textures.

It is important to note that Mithraic banquets were not orgies or profane feasts, but rather serious and reverent religious rituals. The expected atmosphere was one of contemplation, fraternity, and devotion, not excess or licentiousness. Self-control and discipline, fundamental Mithraic virtues, certainly applied to sacred banquets as well, which aimed to strengthen the community and deepen the spiritual experience, and not the mere pursuit of worldly pleasures. Moderation in the consumption of food and drink was likely valued, in line with the ascetic ethic that permeated, to some extent, Mithraism.

The ritual utensils used in Mithraic banquets, such as chalices, paterae (shallow bowls), plates, and jugs, found in some mithraea, reinforce the ritualized nature of these meals. These objects, often decorated with Mithraic symbols or specific shapes, were not common household utensils, but rather sacred instruments intended exclusively for use in cult rituals. The materiality of these ritual objects contributed to the sacralization of the mithraeum space and to the sensory and aesthetic experience of the sacred banquets.

In summary, Mithraic ritual meals and banquets represented crucial moments in the life of the Mithraic community, transcending the mere function of physical sustenance to become sacred acts of communion and fraternity. Held in the mysterious atmosphere of the mithraea, these banquets strengthened social bonds between initiates, fostered a sense of belonging to a cohesive group, and offered symbolic communion with the divine. The food and drink consumed, such as bread and wine, laden with symbolism, and the reverence and discipline that characterized these events demonstrate the central importance of Mithraic banquets in the religious and communal experience of the cult of Mithras.

Chapter 17
Expressions of Devotion

Beyond secret rituals, sacred banquets, and enigmatic symbolism, the religious experience of Mithraism certainly included verbal and performative expressions of devotion intended to invoke deities, praise their deeds, and facilitate communication between the human and divine worlds. Although Mithraism, as a mystery religion, has left few direct textual sources that reveal the details of its liturgy, we can infer the existence of hymns, prayers, and other forms of liturgical expression from indirect evidence, comparisons with contemporary cults, and the very nature of human religious experience, which often manifests through speech and song. Exploring the possible Mithraic liturgy, even hypothetically and conjecturally, is fundamental to understanding the emotional, aesthetic, and performative dimension of the cult of Mithras and how initiates expressed their faith and devotion.

The absence of direct Mithraic liturgical texts is one of the great challenges for reconstructing the cult's liturgy. Unlike other religions of antiquity, such as Christianity or the Egyptian cults, Mithraism did not bequeath to us collections of hymns, prayer books, or liturgical manuals that describe its verbal practices in detail. This absence of primary textual sources can be attributed to the secret nature of the cult, which favored the oral transmission of its mysteries and discretion towards non-initiates. Secrecy, as we have seen, was a central value of Mithraism, and liturgy, as an integral part of the mysteries, was certainly guarded zealously and transmitted only within the initiate community, with no written record for the outside world.

Despite the lack of direct liturgical texts, indirect evidence strongly suggests the existence of verbal and performative expressions of devotion in Mithraism. Firstly, Mithraic iconography offers some clues. In certain representations, Mithraic figures, including Pater and initiates of higher degrees, are shown in attitudes of prayer, with hands raised in gestures of supplication or adoration. These iconographic gestures suggest that personal and collective prayer was part of Mithraic religious practice, even if the exact words of those prayers remain unknown.

Secondly, votive inscriptions found in mithraea, although brief and formulaic, reveal the personal devotion of initiates and their direct relationship with the deities. Dedicatory inscriptions to Mithras, Sol Invictus, and other Mithraic deities, expressing gratitude for graces received or pleas for protection and well-being, demonstrate that initiates communicated with the divine through the written word, even in private and informal contexts. These inscriptions can be interpreted as remnants of more elaborate prayers and verbal liturgical rites that accompanied votive offerings.

Thirdly, comparison with other contemporary mystery cults reinforces the likelihood of the existence of liturgy in Mithraism. Other mystery religions, such as the cults of Isis, Cybele, and Dionysus, had elaborate rituals that involved hymns, prayers, invocations, and chants. It is plausible that Mithraism, inserted in the same religious and cultural context, developed similar liturgical forms, adapted to its theology and specific rites. The very nature of religious experience, in general, tends to express itself through speech and song, as forms of communication with the transcendent and emotional expression of faith.

Fourthly, polemical Christian authors, although hostile to Mithraism, sometimes describe or allude to Mithraic practices that suggest the existence of liturgy. Although these descriptions should be interpreted with caution, given the polemical intent of Christian authors, they may contain remnants of actual observations of Mithraic rituals, which may include verbal liturgical elements. Christian references to oaths, invocations, and forms of Mithraic worship may point to the existence of a liturgy, even if distorted or caricatured from the Christian perspective.

Based on this indirect evidence, we can conjecture about the possible nature of Mithraic liturgy, although we must always acknowledge the speculative character of these reconstructions. It is likely that Mithraic liturgy included hymns, prayers, invocations, and other forms of verbal and performative expression, adapted to the different rituals and degrees of initiation.

Hymns to Mithras and Sol Invictus are highly likely. Given the central place of these deities in the Mithraic pantheon, it is natural that initiates would praise and invoke them through hymns and chants. These hymns could celebrate the mythical deeds of Mithras, such as the Tauroctony and the rock birth, exalt the power and glory of Sol Invictus as the supreme solar deity, and express the devotion and gratitude of the initiates for divine blessings. The hymns could have been sung in chorus, by the whole group of initiates, at specific moments in the rituals, creating an atmosphere of religious exaltation and communal unity. Music, although unknown to us, certainly played an important role in creating the liturgical atmosphere, accompanying the hymns and intensifying the emotional experience of the participants.

Personal and collective prayers were also likely part of Mithraic liturgy. Prayers could have been offered at different times, such as at the beginning or end of rituals, in times of need, or on specific festive dates. Prayers could be of thanksgiving, supplication, praise, or confession, expressing a variety of emotions and religious intentions. Collective prayers, uttered in unison by the whole community, could reinforce the sense of unity and shared faith, while personal prayers, recited individually by initiates, could express their personal devotion and intimate relationship with the deities.

Invocations to other deities of the Mithraic pantheon are equally plausible. In addition to Mithras and Sol Invictus, other deities, such as Cautes and Cautopates, the Moon, and the Ocean, played important roles in Mithraic cosmology and mythology. It is likely that specific invocations were addressed to these deities in particular rituals or at specific times of the year, seeking their protection, blessing, or help in different spheres of life. Invocations could be uttered by priests (such as the Pater) or by initiates of higher degrees, on behalf of the entire community, creating a symbolic link between the human world and the divine pantheon.

In addition to verbal expressions, Mithraic liturgy could have included ritual gestures with devotional meaning. Kneeling worship, prostration, raising hands to heaven, and other bodily gestures could have accompanied prayers and hymns, intensifying the expression of devotion and creating a ritualized body language. Processional movements within the mithraeum, around the Tauroctony relief or other focal points of the ritual space, could also have been part of the liturgy, creating collective ritual movement and reinforcing the sense of communal unity.

The liturgical context for these expressions of devotion could vary. Initiations into different degrees certainly involved specific liturgical rites, adapted to the symbolism of each degree and the candidate's initiatory journey. Sacred banquets could have included hymns and prayers before, during, or after the ritual meal, sacralizing the act of sharing food and promoting spiritual communion. Daily or weekly rituals, performed regularly in mithraea, could have included a more fixed and repetitive liturgy, such as morning and evening prayers, or ritual chants to mark the cycles of time and the divine presence. Special festivals or commemorative dates in the Mithraic calendar, if they existed, could have been celebrated with more solemn and elaborate liturgies, attracting a larger number of initiates and reinforcing the community identity of the cult.

The language of Mithraic liturgy is another open question. Given the international character of Mithraism and the linguistic diversity of the Roman Empire, it is likely that the liturgy was performed in Latin, the lingua franca of the Empire and the language of the Roman military, which constituted a significant segment of the cult's adherents. However, in regions of Greek influence, Greek could also have been used, or perhaps a combination of Latin and Greek. The possibility of vernacular languages being used in local contexts or specific communities cannot be entirely ruled out, although Latin and Greek probably predominated as the main liturgical languages of Mithraism.

In summary, Mithraic liturgy, although shrouded in mystery and absent from direct textual sources, is a fundamental element for understanding the religious experience of the cult of Mithras. The inference of the existence of hymns, prayers, invocations, and ritual gestures, based on indirect evidence and comparison with contemporary cults, allows us to glimpse the devotional and performative dimension of Mithraism. This liturgy, performed in the dark and mysterious mithraea, provided initiates with means to express their faith, communicate with the divine, strengthen community bonds, and experience an intense and transformative religious experience.

Chapter 18
Visual Language of the Cult

In the vast and multifaceted universe of Mithraism, art and iconography emerge as fundamental pillars for understanding the cult, transcending mere decorative function to constitute a powerful visual language. In a mystery cult, where secrecy and initiation were paramount, images assumed an essential communicative role, eloquently conveying mythical narratives, theological principles, ethical values, and esoteric messages in a multifaceted way, even beyond words. Mithraic art, omnipresent in the mithraea, from the imposing reliefs of the Tauroctony to the mural paintings and votive sculptures, was not merely ornamentation, but rather a vehicle for religious communication, a coded visual language that spoke directly to the senses and souls of initiates, shaping their religious experience and deepening their understanding of the mysteries of Mithras. Analyzing Mithraic iconography, unraveling its intrinsic symbolism, and understanding its communicative function is therefore crucial to penetrating the core of the cult of Mithras and unveiling the visual language that echoed in the sacred caves of the Roman Empire.

The centrality of images in Mithraism is evident in the omnipresence of art in mithraea. Unlike other cults of antiquity that focused primarily on written texts or performative rites, Mithraism favored visual expression as the primary means of religious communication. Most mithraea were richly decorated with mythical scenes, divine figures, cosmic symbols, and allegorical representations, transforming the ritual space into a veritable gallery of sacred art. This primacy of images can be explained by the initiatory nature of the cult and the need to communicate complex and esoteric teachings non-verbally and suggestively, appealing to the intuition and contemplation of initiates. The image, in its ambiguity and symbolic richness, allowed messages to be transmitted on multiple levels of understanding, adapting to the initiatory progression of the adepts and reserving the deepest meanings for the higher degrees.

The Tauroctony, the central scene of Mithras slaying the bull, dominates Mithraic iconography, being the most frequent and emblematic representation found in mithraea throughout the Roman Empire. The relief of the Tauroctony, generally positioned in the sanctuary of the mithraeum, above the altar or main niche, imposed itself as the primary visual focus of the ritual space, attracting the gaze and attention of initiates and serving as a synthetic image of Mithraic myth, theology, and soteriology. The complexity of the Tauroctony scene, with its multiplicity of figures, symbols, and details, invited prolonged contemplation and multivocal interpretation, offering a rich field of meditation for initiates and conveying, through visual language, the central messages of the cult.

Beyond the Tauroctony, Mithraic art encompasses a vast repertoire of images and symbols, enriching the visual language of the cult and complementing the message of the central scene. Scenes of Mithras' birth from the rock (petrogenesis), his heroic deeds, the pact with the Sun, the ascension to heaven, and sacred banquets between Mithras and Sol Invictus are frequently represented, narrating the mythical life cycle of Mithras and expanding the understanding of his divinity. Auxiliary deities, such as Cautes and Cautopates, Sol Invictus, the Moon, and the Ocean, are also often personified in Mithraic scenes, demonstrating the complexity of the pantheon and the divine hierarchy of the cult. Cosmic symbols, such as the signs of the zodiac, planets, constellations, winds, and elements, populate Mithraic iconography, reinforcing the cosmic dimension of the cult and its worldview influenced by astrology.

The visual language of Mithraic art is deeply symbolic. Each figure, object, gesture, color, and spatial arrangement in Mithraic representations carries a specific symbolic meaning, contributing to the overall message of the image and the communication of the mysteries of the cult. As we have explored previously, the Phrygian cap, the curved knife, the torch, the bull, the dog, the serpent, the scorpion, the raven, the Sun, the Moon, and the seven-step ladder are just some of the most recurring and significant symbols in Mithraic iconography, each with multiple layers of meaning and complex interpretations debated among scholars. Deciphering this symbolism, understanding the secret language of Mithraic art, is a constant challenge for researchers, but also the key to unlocking the mysteries of the cult of Mithras.

The function of Mithraic art went far beyond mere decoration or illustration of myths. Mithraic art was instrumental to the religious experience of initiates, playing an active role in transmitting the cult's teachings, creating the ritualistic atmosphere of mithraea, and facilitating the spiritual transformation of adepts. First, Mithraic art visually narrated the myths of the cult, making them accessible and vivid for initiates, even for those who did not master reading or writing. The scenes of the Tauroctony and other Mithraic myths, represented in reliefs and paintings, told the sacred story of Mithras, from his birth to his ascension, conveying the foundational events of the cult and reinforcing the religious identity of participants.

Second, Mithraic art communicated theological and cosmological principles visually and symbolically. The Tauroctony scene, for example, condensed the dualistic cosmology of Mithraism, the struggle between the forces of order and chaos, the primordial sacrifice that gave rise to the universe, and Mithras' role as cosmic savior. The representation of planetary spheres, zodiac signs, and other cosmic figures in mithraea illustrated the Mithraic worldview, its understanding of the ordered universe, and the influence of the stars on human life. Mithraic art, in this sense, functioned as a visual manual of the cult's theology and cosmology, offering initiates a graphic representation of their fundamental beliefs.

Third, Mithraic art created the mysterious and ritualistic atmosphere of mithraea. The elaborate decoration of the sacred caves, with mythical scenes, divine figures, and cosmic symbols, transformed the space of the mithraeum into a microcosm of the Mithraic universe, transporting initiates to a sacred world isolated from the profane. The dim and flickering lighting, casting shadows on the decorated walls, intensified the mysterious character of the environment and contributed to the sensory and emotional experience of rituals. Mithraic art, in this sense, created an immersive environment that facilitated introspection, contemplation, and mystical experience for initiates.

Fourth, Mithraic art served as an aid to meditation and contemplation. The complexity of the images, the richness of symbolism, and the multiplicity of levels of meaning in Mithraic representations offered fertile ground for meditation and personal reflection. Initiates could contemplate the mythical scenes, meditate on the meaning of symbols, seek deeper layers of interpretation, and apply Mithraic teachings to their own spiritual lives. Mithraic art, in this sense, stimulated active contemplation and personal engagement of initiates with the mysteries of the cult, leading them to a deeper understanding of their faith and their spiritual journey.

The artistic materials and techniques used in Mithraic art varied according to region, period, and available resources. Stone reliefs, carved in limestone, marble, or other local materials, were the most common and enduring art form in mithraea, especially for representing the Tauroctony and other important mythical scenes. Mural painting, in fresco or tempera, was used to decorate the walls and ceilings of mithraea, filling the spaces with narrative scenes, symbolic figures, and decorative patterns. Round sculpture, although less frequent than reliefs, was used to represent isolated divine figures or sculptural groups, enriching the decoration of mithraea and giving them a three-dimensional dimension. The use of color, especially blue, red, gold, and white, intensified the visual impact of Mithraic art and reinforced its chromatic symbolism.

In summary, Mithraic art and iconography constitute a complex and multifaceted visual language, essential for understanding the cult of Mithras. The Tauroctony, as the central image, and the vast repertoire of mythical scenes, divine figures, and cosmic symbols that populate mithraea, convey narratives, theological principles, and esoteric messages eloquently and suggestively. The function of Mithraic art went far beyond mere decoration, serving as a vehicle for religious communication, an aid to meditation, and a crucial element in creating the ritualistic atmosphere of mithraea. Deciphering the visual language of Mithraic art remains a challenge for scholars, but also an inexhaustible source of knowledge and fascination, revealing the richness and depth of the cult of Mithras and its ability to communicate its mysteries through images and symbols.

Chapter 19
Strength, Sacrifice, and Renewal

In the intricate and multifaceted symbolism of Mithraism, the figure of the bull emerges with a unique prominence and significance, occupying a central place in both the mythical narrative and the iconography of the cult. The bull sacrificed in the Tauroctony, the core scene of Mithraism, is not merely a passive animal in the cosmic drama, but rather a complex and polyvalent symbol, laden with multiple layers of interpretation that reverberate throughout Mithraic theology and cosmology. The symbolism of the bull in Mithraism evokes fundamental concepts such as primal strength, exuberant fertility, primordial sacrifice, necessary death, and cyclical renewal of life, inextricably intertwined with the figure of Mithras and the central message of the cult. Unraveling the symbolism of the bull, exploring its multiple facets, and understanding its importance in the Tauroctony is essential to penetrating the deepest mysteries of Mithraism and grasping the richness of its visual and mythical language.

To fully understand the symbolism of the bull in Mithraism, it is important to situate it within a broader cultural context, considering the ancestral and multifaceted meaning that this robust and imposing animal held in various ancient cultures and religious traditions. Since the Paleolithic, the bull, with its impressive physical strength, its evident virility, and its fundamental role in agriculture and livestock, has been revered as a symbol of power, fertility, vitality, and abundance. In various civilizations of the ancient world, the bull was associated with celestial and terrestrial deities, primordial forces of nature, and cycles of life, death, and renewal, acquiring a complex and multifaceted symbolic status that transcended its mere animal condition.

In Mesopotamia, the bull was associated with celestial deities such as Ishtar and Adad, representing the creative force and fertility of nature. In Ancient Egypt, the Apis bull was venerated as an incarnation of the god Ptah, a symbol of royal power and cyclical renewal. In the Minoan civilization of Crete, the bull played a central role in rituals and ceremonies, such as the famous bull-leaping, representing brute force, agility, and connection with the forces of nature. In Ancient Greece, the bull was consecrated to various deities, such as Zeus, Dionysus, and Poseidon, symbolizing divine power, virility, and oceanic force. In the Roman world, the bull continued to be associated with deities such as Jupiter and Mars, maintaining its connotations of power, military strength, and fecundity.

This ancestral symbolic legacy of the bull, imbued with connotations of strength, fertility, power, and connection with the divine, certainly influenced the adoption and reinterpretation of the bull in the context of Mithraism. The followers of the cult of Mithras, inserted in the Roman world and immersed in a cultural context that valued the bull as a powerful symbol, found in this animal a familiar and resonant visual language, capable of communicating complex and profound messages about the mysteries of their cult.

In Mithraism, the bull assumes a central and multifaceted role in the Tauroctony scene, becoming the passive protagonist of the primordial sacrifice and the vertex of a complex network of symbolisms. In the canonical image of the Tauroctony, Mithras, imposing and resolute, dominates the bull, subduing and stabbing it with a curved knife. The bull, in turn, falls under Mithras' power, bowing in a gesture of surrender and sacrifice. From this sacrifice emanates a primordial life force, represented by the blood gushing from the wound and fertilizing the earth, giving rise to new forms of life. The bull in the Tauroctony is not, therefore, merely a victim, but rather a catalyzing agent of a cosmic process of creation and renewal, its sacrifice being essential for the maintenance of universal order and the perpetuation of the cycle of life.

One of the most evident interpretations of the symbolism of the bull in Mithraism is its association with primal and indomitable strength. The bull, an animal of imposing stature, muscular and with a palpable brute energy, represents the life force in its pure state, the creative energy and generative power of nature. In the Tauroctony, Mithras subdues and dominates this brute force, not to destroy it, but to channel and direct it towards cosmic ends, transforming the chaotic energy of the bull into an ordered and creative force. The sacrifice of the bull, in this sense, can be interpreted as the domestication of primal force by the divine intelligence of Mithras, the imposition of order over chaos, the organization of the cosmos from raw and formless energy. The bull, as a symbol of primal strength, represents the raw material of creation, the vital energy that Mithras shapes and transforms into an ordered universe.

In addition to strength, the bull in Mithraism is also intrinsically linked to the symbolism of fertility and abundance. The bull's virility, its reproductive capacity, and its association with livestock and agriculture make it a natural symbol of fecundity, prosperity, and abundance. In the Tauroctony, the blood of the bull, gushing onto the earth, is described as the source of all plant and animal life, fertilizing the soil and allowing the rebirth of nature. From the blood of the bull are born ears of wheat, vines, and other plants beneficial to humanity, symbolizing the abundance of the fruits of the earth, material prosperity, and the abundance of natural resources. The bull, as a symbol of fertility, represents the source of life and nourishment, the vital principle that ensures the continuity of existence and the prosperity of the created world.

Sacrifice is evidently a central element of the symbolism of the bull in Mithraism, evident in the Tauroctony scene itself. The bull is sacrificed by Mithras in a primordial act that gives rise to the cosmos and renews life. This sacrifice is not an act of cruelty or gratuitous destruction, but rather a necessary and beneficial act, a creative sacrifice that allows the transformation of the bull's raw energy into life and cosmic order. The sacrifice of the bull can be interpreted as a paradigm for the personal and spiritual sacrifice that Mithraic initiates were called to make in their own lives, renouncing their selfish desires and earthly passions to dedicate themselves to the path of light and salvation. The bull, as a symbol of sacrifice, represents the need for renunciation and selflessness to achieve a greater good, spiritual transformation, and union with the divine.

Closely linked to sacrifice is the idea of death and renewal in Mithraic bull symbolism. The bull is killed by Mithras, but from its death comes life. The blood of the bull fertilizes the earth, and its death allows the rebirth of nature and the continuity of the cycle of life. This cycle of death and renewal, present in many ancient myths and religions, is central to the message of Mithraism, which offers a promise of salvation and life after death to its initiates. The bull, as a symbol of death and renewal, represents the transience of earthly life, the inevitability of physical death, but also the hope of resurrection and eternal life in the realm of light, promised to the followers of the cult. The death of the bull in the Tauroctony is not an absolute end, but rather a passage to a new form of existence, a rebirth on a higher plane, echoing the promise of spiritual transformation and immortality offered by Mithraism.

In summary, the symbolism of the bull in Mithraism is multifaceted and rich in layers of meaning. The bull represents primal strength, exuberant fertility, primordial sacrifice, necessary death, and cyclical renewal of life, condensing within itself fundamental concepts of Mithraic theology, cosmology, and soteriology. Its central presence in the Tauroctony scene and its recurrence in other iconographic contexts of the cult underscore its importance as a key symbol for understanding the mysteries of Mithras. Contemplation of the symbolism of the bull, meditation on its multiple facets, and its interpretation in the context of the Mithraic mythical narrative invite a deep immersion in the universe of Mithraism, revealing the secret messages and esoteric teachings that the cult conveyed through the visual language of its art and iconography.

Chapter 20
The Cosmos in the Mithraeum

One of the most fascinating and distinctive aspects of Mithraic art and iconography is the omnipresence of zodiacal symbolism, which permeates the decoration of the mithraea and reveals the profound cosmic worldview that underpinned the cult of Mithras. The twelve signs of the zodiac, recurrently represented in reliefs, paintings, and sculptures, were not mere ornamental elements, but rather keys to a deeper understanding of the Mithraic universe, reflecting the belief in cosmic influence over human destiny, in the celestial order that governs the world, and in the soul's journey through the planetary spheres. The integration of the zodiac into the mithraeum, the subterranean ritual space itself, transformed this sacred place into a microcosm, a miniature representation of the celestial macrocosm, where initiates could symbolically experience their insertion into the cosmic order and their spiritual journey through the heavens. Exploring zodiacal symbolism in Mithraism, unraveling the meaning of the signs within the context of the cult, and understanding their function in the decoration of the mithraea is essential to grasping the complexity and sophistication of the Mithraic worldview.

The integration of the zodiac in Mithraic art and architecture was not an isolated phenomenon, but rather a manifestation of the growing popularity of astrology in the Roman world during the Imperial centuries. The belief in the influence of the stars on terrestrial events and individual destiny spread widely across various layers of Roman society, finding expression in various forms of worship, philosophy, and divination practices. Mithraism, emerging in this cultural context permeated by astrology, naturally incorporated zodiacal symbolism into its belief system and visual language, adapting and reinterpreting the zodiacal signs according to its specific theology and cosmology. The adoption of the zodiac by Mithraism thus reflects its capacity for syncretism and adaptation to the Roman cultural environment, integrating popular elements and currents of thought of the time into its own religious system.

The complete zodiacal cycle, composed of the twelve signs of Aries, Taurus, Gemini, Cancer, Leo, Virgo, Libra, Scorpio, Sagittarius, Capricorn, Aquarius, and Pisces, is recurrently represented in mithraea, generally arranged in circular or semicircular friezes, adorning the vaulted ceilings, entrance arches, or side walls of the ritual spaces. The order of the signs generally follows the traditional astrological sequence, beginning with Aries (the ram) and ending with Pisces (the fish), representing the annual cycle of the sun through the constellations and the progression of cosmic time. The presence of the complete zodiacal cycle in mithraea reinforces the idea of cosmic totality, encompassing the entirety of the ordered universe and its cyclical manifestation in time.

The representation of the zodiacal signs in Mithraic art follows relatively consistent iconographic conventions, albeit with regional and stylistic variations. Each sign is generally represented through its traditional animal or figurative symbol: Aries as a ram, Taurus as a bull, Gemini as twins, Cancer as a crab, Leo as a lion, Virgo as a virgin, Libra as a scale, Scorpio as a scorpion, Sagittarius as a centaur archer, Capricorn as a goat-fish, Aquarius as a water bearer, and Pisces as two fish. These zodiacal symbols were easily recognizable to the Roman observer, integrated into the visual culture and astrological knowledge of the time, facilitating the communication of the cosmic message of Mithraism.

The meaning of the zodiacal signs in Mithraism is multifaceted and complex, intertwining with the cosmology, theology, and soteriology of the cult. On a general level, the zodiac represents the cosmic order established by Mithras, the organization of the universe into celestial spheres, and the influence of the stars on the terrestrial world. The twelve zodiacal signs can be interpreted as dynamic cosmic forces, influencing human destiny, the cycles of nature, and the course of history. The presence of the zodiac in the mithraeum symbolically situates the ritual space within the cosmic order, transforming it into a point of connection between the terrestrial world and the celestial world.

On a more specific level, each zodiacal sign may have been associated with particular qualities, influences, or divinities within the Mithraic system, although detailed information about these associations is fragmentary and speculative. Some scholars propose that the zodiacal signs could have been related to the seven Mithraic grades, corresponding to different stages of the initiatory journey and different levels of esoteric knowledge. Others suggest that the signs could have been associated with the planets and planetary deities of the Mithraic pantheon, reflecting astrological influence on the divine hierarchy and ritual practice.

The association of Taurus with the sacrificial bull of the Tauroctony itself is a particularly evident and relevant interpretation. The sign of Taurus, represented by the bull, is directly linked to the central figure of the Mithraic sacrifice, reinforcing the symbolism of the bull as primordial force, fertility, and renewing sacrifice, as explored in previous pages. The presence of the sign of Taurus in the Mithraic zodiacal cycle may underline the cosmic importance of the Tauroctony sacrifice, situating it as a fundamental event not only in the mythical narrative but also in the structure of the ordered universe, reflected in the zodiac.

The mithraeum, decorated with the zodiacal cycle, is transformed into a microcosm, a small-scale representation of the Mithraic universe. Upon entering the mithraeum and moving within this ritual space, initiates were symbolically inserted into the cosmos, placed under the celestial vault represented by the zodiacal ceiling, and immersed in the cosmic order that governs the world. The mithraeum, as a microcosm, allowed initiates to symbolically experience their connection to the universe, their participation in the cosmic order, and their spiritual journey as a microreproduction of Mithras' cosmic journey.

The arrangement of the zodiac in the mithraeum may also have had ritual and symbolic significance. The placement of the zodiacal cycle on the vaulted ceiling of many mithraea, for example, directly evoked the celestial sphere, the starry firmament that covers the terrestrial world. By looking up during rituals, initiates were confronted with the visual representation of the cosmos, reinforcing their awareness of the vastness of the universe and their insertion into the cosmic order. The arrangement of the zodiac in arches or side friezes could demarcate the boundaries of the sacred space, separating the mithraeum from the profane world and creating a symbolic border between the ritual microcosm and the celestial macrocosm.

Zodiacal symbolism in Mithraism is also intrinsically linked to the cult's understanding of time and cosmic cycles. The zodiac, as a visual representation of the annual cycle of the sun through the constellations, embodies the passage of time, the repetition of natural cycles, and the eternity of the cosmos. The presence of the zodiac in mithraea may have served to mark ritual time, indicating festive dates, auspicious moments for certain rites, or the progression of the seasons. The zodiac, in this sense, rhythmically punctuated Mithraic religious life, synchronizing the cult's rituals with cosmic cycles and reinforcing their connection to the natural order of the universe.

Astrological influence is a key element to understanding zodiacal symbolism in Mithraism.

Astrology, as a system of beliefs and practices that attribute meaning and influence to the stars, permeated the religious and cultural thought of the Roman world, and Mithraism was no exception. The integration of the zodiac into Mithraic iconography reflects the cult's adoption of astrological principles, the belief in the influence of planets and constellations on human destiny, and the search for an astrological understanding of the universe and divinity. The soul's journey through the planetary spheres, a central theme of Mithraic cosmology, is directly related to astrology, representing the soul's ascension through planetary influences and its liberation from the forces of fate.

In conclusion, zodiacal symbolism in Mithraism is a complex and multifaceted visual language that enriches the art, architecture, and religious experience of the cult. The complete zodiacal cycle, represented in mithraea, transforms the ritual space into a microcosm of the universe, reflecting the cosmic worldview of Mithraism and its belief in the influence of the stars on human destiny. The presence of the zodiac in mithraea reinforces the idea of cosmic order, temporal cycles, and the insertion of initiates into a vast and ordered universe. Deciphering zodiacal symbolism in Mithraism, understanding the meaning of the signs in the context of the cult, and analyzing their function in the decoration of mithraea offer a fascinating glimpse into the complexity and sophistication of the Mithraic worldview, and the way in which the cult of Mithras communicated its mysteries through the visual language of its art and iconography.

Chapter 21
Symbolism of Light and Darkness

One of the most distinctive theological and cosmological pillars of Mithraism is its cosmic dualism, the fundamental belief in a primordial and perpetual struggle between opposing forces that shape the universe and human existence. This dualism, intrinsic to the Mithraic worldview, finds powerful visual expression in the symbolism of light and darkness, which permeates the art, iconography, and liturgy of the cult. The binary opposition between light and darkness, represented through a rich variety of images, symbols, and allegories, is not merely an aesthetic element in the decoration of mithraea, but rather a fundamental visual language for communicating the dualistic nature of the cosmos, the eternal conflict between good and evil, the soul's journey from darkness to light, and the promise of salvation offered by Mithraism. Exploring the symbolism of light and darkness in Mithraism, unraveling its multiple representations, and understanding its relationship to cosmic dualism is crucial to grasping the essence of Mithraic theology and its central soteriological message.

Cosmic dualism in Mithraism manifests itself in various forms and levels, reflecting a worldview that perceives the universe as a stage for an incessant struggle between antagonistic principles. This primordial struggle opposes, in general terms, the forces of order, light, and good to the forces of chaos, darkness, and evil, a duality that is reflected both in Mithraic cosmology (the organization of the universe into celestial and chthonic spheres) and in anthropology (the human condition as a battleground between spiritual and material impulses). Mithraism, in this sense, inherits and reinterprets dualistic traditions present in Persian and Iranian religions, adapting them to the Roman context and integrating them into its own system of beliefs and practices.

The symbolism of light and darkness becomes the most eloquent visual translation of this cosmic dualism in Mithraism. Light, with its connotations of clarity, knowledge, order, good, and divinity, is opposed to darkness, associated with obscurity, ignorance, chaos, evil, and chthonic forces. This binary opposition, deeply rooted in human experience and the observation of the natural cycles of day and night, becomes a powerful metaphor for the cosmic struggle between good and evil, visually expressing the dualistic theology of Mithraism. The language of light and darkness, familiar and resonant to the Roman audience, allowed for the effective and suggestive communication of the fundamental principles of the cult of Mithras through art and iconography.

The very architecture of the mithraeum, the subterranean sacred cave, contributes to the symbolism of light and darkness. The mithraeum, immersed in darkness, illuminated only by the flickering light of lamps and torches, evokes the chthonic world, the depths of the earth, and the realm of darkness. The narrow, descending entrance to the mithraeum symbolizes the journey to the underworld, the plunge into darkness before the quest for spiritual light. The interior of the mithraeum, contrasting with the sunlit outer world, creates a liminal space, a place of transition between the profane world of light and the sacred world of darkness, where initiation and spiritual transformation become possible.

Within the mithraeum, ritual lighting, carefully controlled through lamps and torches, plays a crucial role in creating the mysterious atmosphere and intensifying the symbolism of light and darkness. The flickering light, casting shadows on the decorated walls, animates the mythical images, giving them a dynamic and immersive dimension. The contrast between light and shadow, accentuated by artificial lighting, visually reinforces cosmic dualism, creating an environment where the struggle between light and darkness becomes palpable and experiential. The very quest for light within the dark space of the mithraeum can be interpreted as a metaphor for the initiatory journey, the quest for spiritual enlightenment through the mysteries of Mithras, leaving the darkness of ignorance and entering the light of divine knowledge.

Mithraic iconography explores the symbolism of light and darkness in various ways, utilizing images, figures, and allegories that visually represent this fundamental opposition. The figure of Mithras himself, often depicted radiating light and energy, embodies the principle of light, the agent of cosmic order, and the bearer of spiritual enlightenment. Sol Invictus, the supreme solar deity of the Mithraic pantheon, represents the primordial source of divine light, the celestial star that illuminates the world and overcomes the darkness of night. The torch, one of the most recurring symbols of Mithraic iconography, embodies the light of knowledge, truth, and hope, guiding initiates on the path of initiation and illuminating their spiritual journey.

In contrast to light, darkness is often represented more implicitly and symbolically in Mithraic iconography than through personified figures of evil or darkness. The darkness of the mithraeum, as a subterranean ritual space, already evokes the realm of darkness and the chthonic world. Certain animals, such as the serpent and the scorpion, present in the Tauroctony scene and other Mithraic contexts, can be associated with the chthonic and obscure forces of nature, representing the dark and chaotic aspects of the universe. The bull itself, in its chthonic and primordial dimension, can be interpreted as a manifestation of the raw, unformed energy of darkness, which needs to be subdued and transformed by the light of Mithras' divine intelligence.

The figures of Cautes and Cautopates, Mithras' companions often depicted in Mithraic reliefs, particularly eloquently embody the symbolism of light and darkness. Cautes, carrying a raised torch, symbolizes the rising sun, increasing light, day, and life. Cautopates, carrying an inverted torch, symbolizes the setting sun, decreasing light, night, and death. The duality of Cautes and Cautopates, representing the ascent and descent of the sun, light and darkness, day and night, visually condenses the fundamental cosmic cycle of light and darkness and their eternal alternation in the universe. Their constant presence in Mithraic iconography, often flanking the Tauroctony scene or other representations of Mithras, reinforces the centrality of the light-darkness dualism in the Mithraic worldview.

The arrangement of Cautes and Cautopates in Mithraic reliefs also carries symbolic meaning. Cautes, with the raised torch, is generally placed to the right of Mithras, the side of light, the rising sun, and the celestial hemisphere. Cautopates, with the inverted torch, is generally placed to the left of Mithras, the side of darkness, the setting sun, and the chthonic hemisphere. This spatial arrangement, consistent in many representations, visually reinforces the polarity between light and darkness and their association with the celestial and chthonic hemispheres of the Mithraic universe. The very central position of Mithras, between Cautes and Cautopates, can symbolize his role as mediator between light and darkness, the agent that balances the opposing forces of the cosmos and guarantees universal order.

The light-darkness dualism in Mithraism is not limited to a mere cosmological description but also has a profound ethical and soteriological dimension. The cosmic struggle between light and darkness is reflected in the inner struggle of the human soul, the conflict between spiritual and material impulses, between good and evil that resides within each individual. The Mithraic initiatory path, the journey through the grades, is often interpreted as a gradual progression from darkness to light, a process of spiritual purification and ascension of the soul towards the realm of divine light. The promise of Mithraic salvation, the hope for a more auspicious afterlife in the celestial realm, is often expressed in terms of ascension to light, liberation from the darkness of ignorance and suffering, and union with the primordial source of divine light.

Mithraic ethics, valuing virtues such as discipline, loyalty, courage, and self-control, can be interpreted as a constant struggle against the forces of darkness within oneself. Adherence to the moral precepts of Mithraism, the practice of rituals, and progression through the initiatory grades represent a continuous effort to strengthen the inner light, to overcome the dark tendencies of human nature, and to align oneself with the forces of order and good in the cosmos. The Mithraic ideal of the perfect initiate is one who has achieved spiritual enlightenment, who has overcome the darkness of ignorance and evil, and who has become an agent of light in the world, reflecting the order and harmony of the Mithraic universe.

In conclusion, the symbolism of light and darkness in Mithraism constitutes a powerful and multifaceted visual language that communicates the essence of cosmic dualism and the soteriological message of the cult. The binary opposition between light and darkness, expressed through the architecture of the mithraea, ritual lighting, the iconography of the Tauroctony, and the figures of Cautes and Cautopates, permeates the entire Mithraic religious experience, reinforcing the belief in the primordial struggle between good and evil and the soul's journey from darkness to light. Deciphering this dualistic symbolism, understanding its multiple representations, and its relationship to Mithraic theology and ethics offer a fascinating glimpse into the depth and complexity of the Mithraic worldview and the way in which the cult of Mithras communicated its mysteries through the visual language of light and darkness.

Chapter 22
Other Symbolic Animals in Mithraism

While the bull dominates the symbolic bestiary of Mithraism, occupying the center of the Tauroctony scene and radiating its multifaceted meaning throughout the cult, the Mithraic iconographic universe is populated by a rich variety of other symbolic animals, each with its specific load of meaning and its contribution to the complexity of the visual language of Mithraism. Besides the bull, the lion, the serpent, the scorpion, and the raven emerge as recurring animal figures in Mithraic art, present in various mythical scenes, rituals, and decorations of the Mithraea, enriching the symbolic bestiary of the cult and conveying additional messages about Mithraic cosmology, theology, and soteriology. Exploring the symbolism of these other animals, unveiling their multiple layers of meaning, and understanding their function in the context of Mithraism is essential to complete the panorama of the Mithraic symbolic bestiary and to appreciate the richness and sophistication of its visual language.

The lion, an imposing, majestic, and solar animal par excellence, occupies a prominent place among the symbolic animals of Mithraism, often associated with strength, power, royalty, and the solar divinity itself.

The presence of the lion in Mithraic iconography is not as omnipresent as that of the bull, but in certain contexts, such as in initiation rituals and representations of solar deities, the lion assumes a relevant symbolic role, reinforcing the solar and hierarchical dimension of Mithraism. The association of the lion with the Sun is a recurring theme in various ancient cultures, and Mithraism inherits and reinterprets this connection, integrating the lion into its solar and cosmic symbolism.

The initiatory degree of Leo (Lion), the fourth degree in the Mithraic hierarchy, testifies to the symbolic importance of the lion in the cult. Initiation into this degree certainly involved rites and symbols associated with the lion, although the precise details remain unknown due to initiatory secrecy. It is plausible that initiates who reached the degree of Leo were invested with symbolic attributes of the lion, such as courage, strength, and authority, identifying with the solar and regal qualities associated with this animal. The passage to the degree of Leo could be interpreted as a symbolic ascension to a higher level of spiritual power and esoteric knowledge, bringing the initiate closer to the divine and solar sphere.

Iconographically, the lion appears in various Mithraic scenes, often associated with Mithras or Sol Invictus. In some representations of the Tauroctony, a lion accompanies the scene, licking the blood of the bull or participating in some way in the cosmic drama. In other images, Mithras is represented dominating a lion or riding on a lion, reinforcing his power over the forces of nature and his connection with leonine symbolism.

Sol Invictus, the supreme solar deity of the Mithraic pantheon, is also sometimes represented with leonine attributes, such as the lion's skin or accompanied by this animal, underlining its solar nature and its ruling power over the cosmos.

The symbolism of the lion in Mithraism can be interpreted on multiple levels. On a cosmic level, the lion can represent the Sun at its zenith, the maximum solar force, the power of light that overcomes darkness. Its association with fire and heat reinforces its solar dimension and its connection with the vital energy of the cosmos. On a soteriological level, the lion can symbolize the spiritual strength, moral courage, and determination necessary to travel the Mithraic initiatory path and to achieve salvation. The lion, as king of the animals, represents the ideal of power and self-mastery that Mithraic initiates aspired to achieve through their spiritual journey.

The serpent, in contrast to the solar and celestial lion, assumes a more chthonic, terrestrial, and ambivalent symbolism in Mithraism, associated with both the earth and regeneration as well as with obscure and mysterious forces. The presence of the serpent in the Tauroctony scene, where it crawls towards the sacrificed bull, drinking its blood or biting its testicles, suggests an ambiguous and complex role of this animal in the Mithraic context. The serpent, a creature that lives underground, crawls on the earth, and sheds its skin, carries connotations of chthonicity, regeneration, transformation, and mystery, which are explored in Mithraic symbolism.

The association of the serpent with the earth and chthonic forces is evident in its representation in the Tauroctony, where it emerges from the ground to approach the sacrificed bull. The serpent, as a terrestrial creature, personifies the forces of the earth, the fertility of the soil, and the vital energy that emanates from the underworld. Its presence in the sacrifice scene may indicate that the serpent benefits from the vital energy released by the death of the bull, receiving and channeling the regenerative force that emanates from the primordial sacrifice. In this interpretation, the serpent is not necessarily a negative or evil figure, but rather an integral part of the cycle of life and renewal, benefiting from the sacrifice and ensuring the continuity of earthly fertility.

The regenerative symbolism of the serpent is also present in its ability to shed its skin, a natural process that has been interpreted in various cultures as a symbol of rebirth, renewal, and transformation. In Mithraism, the serpent can represent the spiritual transformation capacity of the initiate, their journey of symbolic death and rebirth to a new level of existence through initiation. The serpent, in this sense, personifies the potential for inner renewal, the ability to leave behind the old and embrace the new, a central theme in Mithraic soteriology.

However, the serpent also carries obscure and mysterious connotations in Mithraic symbolism, echoing its ambivalent reputation in other religious traditions. Its chthonic nature, its connection with the underworld, and its potential venom associate the serpent with unknown, dangerous, and even malignant forces. In some interpretations, the serpent in the Tauroctony may represent the forces of chaos and disorder that oppose the cosmic order established by Mithras, trying to benefit from the primordial sacrifice to disrupt the balance of the universe. This ambivalence of the serpent's symbolism reflects the complexity of the Mithraic worldview, which recognizes the presence of obscure and ambiguous forces in nature and human existence, even within the process of creation and renewal.

The scorpion, another frequent animal in the Tauroctony scene, assumes a more unequivocally chthonic symbolism associated with death and pain. The scorpion, a terrestrial, venomous, and nocturnal creature, personifies the destructive forces of nature, the venom of death, and the darkness of the underworld. Its presence in the Tauroctony, pinching the testicles of the bull, suggests a negative and obstructive role in the sacrifice process, trying to prevent the fertility and regeneration that should emanate from the death of the bull. The scorpion, in this context, can represent the forces of evil and chaos that oppose Mithras' divine plan, trying to frustrate cosmic creation and renewal.

The symbolism of the scorpion in Mithraism is often associated with death, suffering, and pain. Its venomous sting, capable of inflicting a painful and potentially fatal sting, makes the scorpion a natural symbol of mortality, danger, and destructive forces. In the Tauroctony, the scorpion, by attacking the reproductive organs of the bull, symbolizes castration, infertility, and the interruption of the cycle of life, directly opposing the symbolism of fertility and renewal associated with the blood of the bull. The scorpion, in this sense, represents the forces of death and sterility that threaten the cosmic order and the continuity of life.

On a psychological and soteriological level, the scorpion can represent the dark aspects of human nature, destructive passions, selfish impulses, and the temptation of evil. The fight against the scorpion within oneself, the effort to overcome negative tendencies and dark desires, can be interpreted as part of the Mithraic initiatory journey, the need to face and overcome inner darkness to achieve spiritual light. The scorpion, in this context, personifies the obstacles and challenges that the initiate must overcome on the path of initiation, the temptations and dangers that threaten to divert the seeker of truth from their ultimate goal.

The raven, the last of the symbolic birds to explore in this Mithraic bestiary, assumes a more ambivalent and multifaceted role, associated with both divine messaging and esoteric knowledge as well as with funereal and chthonic connotations. The presence of the raven in the Tauroctony scene, often pecking at the bull or drinking its blood, suggests a role as an intermediary between worlds, a messenger that connects the earthly plane with the divine, or perhaps a psychopomp that guides souls to the afterlife. The raven's black color, its necrophagous diet, and its mysterious behavior contribute to its ambivalent aura and the richness of its symbolism in Mithraism.

The initiatory degree of Corax (Raven), the first degree in the Mithraic hierarchy, indicates the symbolic importance of the raven at the beginning of the initiatory journey. Initiates of the Corax degree, the novices in the cult, may have been associated with the symbolism of the raven as messengers, apprentices, and seekers of knowledge. The raven, as a messenger bird, could represent the role of the Corax initiate as a receiver and transmitter of the cult's messages, the first step in the journey of unraveling the mysteries of Mithras. Initiation into the Corax degree could be interpreted as a call to the search for esoteric knowledge, the beginning of the spiritual journey towards enlightenment, guided by the ancestral wisdom of the raven.

The association of the raven with divine messages can also be interpreted in the context of the Tauroctony. The presence of the raven in the sacrifice scene may indicate that it is a messenger sent by the celestial deities to communicate some divine design related to the sacrifice of the bull. The raven could be the bearer of a divine order for Mithras to perform the sacrifice, or the announcer of the cosmic and beneficial consequences that will emanate from the Tauroctony. In this interpretation, the raven is not just an animal that participates in the scene, but rather an agent of the divine will, transmitting a crucial message for the unfolding of the cosmic drama.

The raven's funereal and chthonic connotations may also be relevant to its symbolism in Mithraism. The raven, as a necrophagous bird associated with death and battlefields, can represent the passage between life and death, the soul's journey to the underworld, and the transience of earthly existence. Its presence in the Tauroctony could evoke the sacrificial and soteriological dimension of the cult, the promise of life after death, and the hope of salvation offered by Mithraism. The raven, in this sense, guides the souls of initiates on their journey to the afterlife, leading them through the darkness of death to the light of eternal life.

In summary, the symbolic bestiary of Mithraism, besides the central bull, is enriched by other animals such as the lion, the serpent, the scorpion, and the raven, each with its specific load of meaning and its contribution to the complexity of the visual language of the cult. The lion represents solar strength and divine power, the serpent chthonic ambivalence and regeneration, the scorpion destructive forces and death, and the raven divine messaging and esoteric knowledge. Understanding the symbolism of these animals, their interaction in Mithraic iconography, and their relationship with the theology and soteriology of the cult deeply enrich our apprehension of the mysteries of Mithras and the richness of its visual language.

Chapter 23
Symbolism of Ritual Objects

In the mysterious ceremonial of Mithraism, besides the mythical images and cosmic symbols, ritual objects played a crucial role, materializing the beliefs, practices, and religious experience of the cult. These instruments, carefully crafted and imbued with symbolic meaning, were not mere scenic props, but rather sacred tools, mediators between the human and divine worlds, vehicles of ritual action, and bearers of esoteric messages. The curved knife (or short sword), the torch, the chalice (or cup), and the paterae (shallow dishes) stand out among the most prominent and recurring ritual objects in Mithraic iconography and archaeological finds, each with its specific symbolism and particular ritual function. Unveiling the symbolism of Mithraic ritual objects, exploring the meaning of the knife, torch, chalice, and other instruments, and understanding their use in ritual practices is essential to appreciate the materiality of the cult of Mithras and the way in which sacred objects contributed to the religious experience of initiates.

The use of ritual objects is a common feature of various religions and spiritual practices, from the oldest to the contemporary. Sacred objects, such as cult instruments, amulets, offerings, or ritual vessels, serve as bridges between the material world and the spiritual world, condensing in themselves symbolic power, religious meaning, and transcendent force. The materiality of ritual objects, their shape, the materials from which they are made, their decoration, and their use in specific ritual contexts communicate non-verbal messages that complement and enrich the religious experience of participants. In the context of mystery cults, such as Mithraism, ritual objects acquire an even more esoteric and secrecy-laden dimension, functioning as keys to access hidden knowledge and as instruments of initiatory transformation.

The curved knife (or short sword), often depicted in Mithras' hands in the Tauroctony scene, and also present in other Mithraic mythical and ritual scenes, emerges as one of the most symbolic and multifaceted ritual objects of the cult. The knife, in its primordial function as a cutting instrument, naturally evokes the idea of separation, division, and sacrifice. In the context of the Tauroctony, Mithras' knife is the instrument of the primordial sacrifice of the bull, the foundational act that gives rise to the cosmos and allows the renewal of life. The knife, in this sense, symbolizes the creative and transformative power of sacrifice, the ability to generate order from chaos through an act of separation and division.

The curved shape of the Mithraic knife, distinctive in many representations, may also carry specific symbolism, although interpretations vary. Some scholars suggest that the curved shape of the knife could evoke the sickle, an agricultural instrument associated with harvest and fertility, linking the sacrifice of the Tauroctony not only to death, but also to the abundance of the fruits of the earth that emanate from the sacrifice. Others propose that the curve of the knife could have lunar connotations, associating it with the lunar divinity and the cycle of the moon, reinforcing the cosmic and cyclical dimension of Mithraic sacrifice. In some representations, Mithras wields not a curved knife, but a short sword, which may indicate regional or chronological variations in the symbolism of the instrument, or perhaps a different emphasis on the martial aspect and warrior power of Mithras.

The use of the knife in Mithraic rituals, beyond the mythical representation of the Tauroctony, is inferred from some archaeological and iconographic evidence, although the precise details remain unknown. It is plausible that ritual knives were used in initiation ceremonies, perhaps symbolizing the separation of the initiate from the profane world and their entry into the sacred space of the Mithraeum. Knives could also have been used in rites of symbolic sacrifice, offerings, or libations, representing the continuity of the primordial sacrifice of the Tauroctony and the renewal of the alliance between initiates and Mithraic deities. The very possession of a ritual knife could have been a symbol of status and initiatory power, reserved for certain degrees of the Mithraic hierarchy, reinforcing the idea of the knife as a sacred instrument and vehicle of spiritual power.

The torch, another prominent ritual object in Mithraic iconography, especially in the hands of Cautes and Cautopates, but also often associated with Mithras himself, symbolizes light, enlightenment, knowledge, truth, and hope. The torch, as a source of artificial light, opposed to natural darkness, represents the search for spiritual light, the path of initiation as a journey from darkness to light, and the promise of divine illumination offered by Mithraism. The torch, in its flaming flame, also evokes the purifying and transformative fire, the vital energy and spiritual force that guide and protect the initiate on their journey.

The torches carried by Cautes and Cautopates, in their duality and opposition, enrich the symbolism of the torch in Mithraism. Cautes, with the torch raised, symbolizes the ascending light, the rising sun, hope, new beginnings, and the promise of enlightenment. Cautopates, with the torch inverted, symbolizes the descending light, the setting sun, the end of a cycle, the passage to night, and the need for introspection. The duality of the torches, representing the ascent and descent of light, day and night, life and death, condenses the fundamental cosmic cycle of light and darkness, and the initiatory journey as an alternation between moments of illumination and moments of obscurity, of knowledge and mystery.

The use of torches in Mithraic rituals is corroborated by archaeological evidence, namely the discovery of torch holders and lamps in Mithraea, and by the frequent iconographic representation of torches in the hands of ritual figures. Lighted torches certainly illuminated the dark space of the Mithraeum during rituals, creating a mysterious and reverent atmosphere, and intensifying the symbolism of light and darkness. Torches could have been used in ritual processions within the Mithraeum, guiding initiates on their symbolic journey and marking important moments of the ceremony. The passing of the lit torch between initiates could have been a rite of communion and sharing of spiritual light, reinforcing fraternal bonds and the sense of belonging to the Mithraic community.

The chalice (or cup), although less omnipresent in Mithraic iconography than the knife and torch, emerges as a significant ritual object, especially in scenes of sacred banquets and in contexts that evoke communion and ritual sharing of drinks. The chalice, as a container for precious liquids, is naturally associated with the symbolism of ritual drinking, libation, communal sharing, and communion with the divine. In the context of Mithraic banquets, the chalice can represent the container of the sacred wine, the ritually significant drink shared among initiates as an act of communion and fraternity, and possibly as a symbolic representation of the blood of the sacrificed bull or the nectar of immortality.

The iconography of Mithras and Sol Invictus sharing a sacred banquet often includes the representation of a chalice or cup between the two deities, suggesting the ritual and symbolic importance of this object in Mithraic banquets. The chalice, in this context, personifies the act of sharing the ritual drink, the gesture of communion and fraternity between the deities and, by extension, between the initiates who replicated the sacred banquet in the Mithraeum. The chalice, as a container of the drink of immortality, could also evoke the promise of salvation and eternal life offered by Mithraism, symbolizing the final reward of initiates who traveled the path of initiation and achieved union with the divine.

The paterae (shallow dishes), found archaeologically in some Mithraea, and sometimes depicted in iconographic scenes, suggest the use of ritual vessels for libations and offerings. The paterae, due to their shallow and open shape, are particularly suitable for pouring liquids on the altar or on the ground, a common ritual act in various ancient religions as a form of offering to deities, chthonic spirits, or the dead. In Mithraism, paterae could have been used in libations of wine, milk, honey, or water, symbolically offering these precious substances to the Mithraic deities, as an act of devotion, gratitude, or supplication.

In addition to the knife, torch, and chalice, other ritual objects could have been used in Mithraism, although the evidence is more fragmentary and speculative. Censers could have been used to burn incense during rituals, purifying the space and creating a mystical and reverent olfactory atmosphere. Bells or chimes could have been used to mark important ritual moments, such as the beginning or end of a ceremony, or to accompany ritual chants and hymns. Crowns or wreaths of flowers could have been used to adorn initiates on special occasions, symbolizing their purity, consecration, or ascension to a new initiatory degree.

The very ritual attire of initiates, with specific colors and symbols associated with each degree, could be considered a ritual object laden with symbolic meaning, contributing to the ritual experience and Mithraic collective identity.

In conclusion, the symbolism of ritual objects in Mithraism is vast and multifaceted, enriching the visual language and ritual experience of the cult. The knife, the torch, the chalice, and other sacred instruments were not mere props, but ritual tools imbued with symbolic power, mediating communication with the divine, facilitating ritual action, and conveying esoteric messages to initiates. Understanding the symbolism of these ritual objects, their function in the cult's practices, and their materiality as tangible elements of the Mithraic faith are essential to appreciate the richness and complexity of Mithraism and to unravel the mysteries that echoed in the sacred caves of the Roman Empire. In the next part of the book, we will explore the complex and sometimes conflicting relationship between Mithraism and Christianity, the religion that would eventually become dominant in the Roman world, and the factors that led to the gradual decline of the cult of Mithras.

Chapter 24
The Rise of Christianity in the Roman Empire

In the multifaceted and dynamic religious landscape of the Roman Empire, Mithraism did not flourish in isolation, but rather in a context of intense competition and exchange with other cults and beliefs. Among these, Christianity, initially a minority and peripheral movement, gradually emerged as a formidable religious competitor, challenging the popularity of Mithraism and eventually eclipsing it in influence and number of followers. The rise of Christianity in the Roman Empire, a complex and multifaceted phenomenon that unfolded over centuries, represents one of the great turning points in the religious history of the Western world, marking the end of the era of pagan mystery religions and the beginning of Christian hegemony. Understanding the rise of Christianity as a competitor to Mithraism, analyzing the factors that contributed to its success, and identifying the differences and similarities between the two cults is essential to contextualize the decline of Mithraism and to understand the dynamics of religious competition in the late Roman Empire.

The emergence of Christianity in the first century AD, in the eastern provinces of the Roman Empire, marked the beginning of a religious movement that, in a few centuries, would transform the religious and cultural landscape of the Western world. Initially a small group of followers of Jesus of Nazareth, Christianity, driven by apostolic preaching, the dissemination of scriptures, and the gradual conversion of new adherents, progressively expanded throughout the Roman Empire, reaching different social strata, geographical regions, and cultural communities. Despite facing periods of persecution and opposition from Roman authorities, Christianity demonstrated remarkable resilience and adaptability, growing in numbers and influence until it became, in the fourth century AD, the dominant religion of the Roman Empire, under Emperor Constantine and his successors.

The growing popularity of Christianity in the Roman Empire can be attributed to a complex combination of factors that interacted synergistically to drive its expansion and consolidation. First, the message of Christianity, centered on the figure of Jesus Christ as savior, universal love, the promise of eternal life, and the resurrection of the dead, resonated with the spiritual and existential needs of many inhabitants of the Roman world, in a period of social transformations, political crises, and religious insecurity. The promise of personal salvation, forgiveness of sins, and a glorious future in the kingdom of God offered comfort, hope, and meaning to individuals who felt disillusioned with traditional civic religions and the elitist philosophies of the time.

Second, the community structure of Christianity, based on local churches, mutual assistance among members, the practice of charity, and support for the needy, attracted individuals seeking social belonging, solidarity, and practical support. Christian communities, organized around bishops and presbyters, offered a space for fellowship, sharing, and mutual aid, in contrast to the relative impersonality and formality of Roman civic religions. The appeal to equality among believers, transcending social and ethnic distinctions, and the inclusion of women, slaves, and marginalized people in the Christian community contributed to the popularity of Christianity in various segments of Roman society.

Third, the effectiveness of Christian preaching and propaganda, driven by itinerant missionaries, the production and dissemination of sacred texts (such as the Gospels and Epistles), and the use of sophisticated methods of persuasion and argumentation, played a crucial role in the expansion of Christianity. The apostles and their successors, traveling throughout the Roman Empire, proclaimed the Christian message in urban centers, rural villages, and Jewish communities of the diaspora, using the Greek language, the lingua franca of the Eastern Roman world, to communicate their message to a vast and diverse audience. The ability of Christian apologists to defend the Christian faith before pagan intellectuals, to respond to criticisms and accusations, and to present Christianity as a superior philosophy and a morally elevated religion contributed to its credibility and to the conversion of members of the Roman elites.

Fourth, the message of religious exclusivity of Christianity, which proclaimed the uniqueness of God and the singularity of Jesus Christ as the only way to salvation, represented a break with the syncretism and religious tolerance characteristic of the Roman world. While Mithraism and other pagan religions easily integrated into the Roman pantheon, accepting the coexistence of various deities and cults, Christianity rejected pagan polytheism and affirmed the falsehood of all other gods, demanding exclusive and total adherence to Christ and his Church. This message of exclusivity, although initially limiting, eventually proved to be a factor of strength, consolidating Christian identity, strengthening the commitment of the faithful, and drawing a clear boundary between Christianity and paganism.

Christianity, in ascending as a formidable religious competitor, presented direct challenges to Mithraism, disputing the same religious ground, attracting similar segments of the Roman population, and offering alternative answers to the same spiritual and existential needs. Although there is no evidence of direct and violent confrontations between Mithraists and Christians on a large scale (unlike Christian persecution by Roman authorities), the religious competition between the two cults was real and significant, manifesting itself in various forms of rivalry and dispute for faithful.

Christianity and Mithraism competed for the same audience, especially in urban centers, military communities, and the middle and lower social strata of

Roman society. Both cults attracted individuals seeking a more personal and emotional religious experience, in contrast to the coldness and formalism of traditional civic religions. Both offered initiation rites, promises of salvation and life after death, rigorous ethical codes, and cohesive community structures. The overlap in target audience and religious offerings made competition between Christianity and Mithraism inevitable, generating a dynamic of rivalry and dispute for faithful.

Christianity, with its message of universal love, forgiveness of sins, and resurrection, presented an attractive alternative to Mithraism, which, despite its popularity, could be perceived as more esoteric, restrictive, and focused on military virtues and rigid discipline. The figure of Jesus Christ, with his palpable humanity, his history of suffering and sacrifice, and the promise of divine love and compassion, could resonate more deeply with some individuals than the mythical and distant figure of Mithras. The Christian message of equality and inclusion, transcending social and ethnic barriers, could attract those who felt excluded or marginalized in Roman society, in contrast to the hierarchical and possibly more restrictive structure of Mithraism.

The flexibility and adaptability of Christianity also gave it competitive advantages over Mithraism. From its beginnings, Christianity demonstrated a remarkable ability to adapt to different cultural and social contexts, incorporating elements of Greek philosophy, Roman culture, and local religious traditions, while maintaining its identity and core message. This capacity for selective syncretism allowed Christianity to gain adherence in various regions of the Roman Empire, adapting its message and practices to the needs and sensibilities of different social and ethnic groups. Mithraism, although it also demonstrated some capacity for regional adaptation, seemed to be less flexible and more attached to a relatively fixed set of rites and myths, which may have limited its capacity for expansion and adaptation to new contexts.

In short, the rise of Christianity represented a formidable religious competitor for Mithraism in the Roman Empire, disputing the same audience, offering alternative answers to the same spiritual and existential needs, and benefiting from competitive advantages in terms of message, community structure, and adaptability. The competition between the two cults, although not always direct and violent, played a crucial role in the religious dynamics of the late Roman world, contributing to the gradual decline of Mithraism and the final triumph of Christianity as the dominant religion of the Empire.

Chapter 25
Mithraism and Christianity

The emergence and expansion of Christianity in the Roman Empire placed it on a collision course, and simultaneously in parallel, with various other religious currents of the time, among which Mithraism stood out. The comparison between Mithraism and Christianity reveals a complex and fascinating parallel, marked by surprising similarities in some aspects, but also by crucial differences that would ultimately determine the fate of each cult in the context of the late Roman world. Exploring this parallel, identifying the points of convergence and divergence between Mithraism and Christianity, is essential to understand not only the dynamics of religious competition in the Roman Empire, but also to appreciate the distinctive characteristics of each cult and the underlying reasons for the eventual triumph of one and the decline of the other. The comparative analysis reveals that, although they shared common ground in terms of spiritual needs and forms of religious expression, theological, structural, and contextual differences were decisive in defining their divergent historical paths.

The similarities between Mithraism and Christianity, which sometimes surprise and intrigue scholars, stem in part from the fact that both are considered mystery religions that flourished in the same cultural and historical environment of the Roman Empire. Both cults offered an initiatory path, marked by secret rites, esoteric teachings, and a gradual progression through hierarchical degrees, promising their adherents a transformative religious experience and a superior knowledge of divine mysteries. This common mystical nature created a shared religious language, with ritual, symbolic, and conceptual elements that resembled each other and facilitated understanding and comparison between the two cults.

One of the most notable points of convergence is the promise of salvation and a more auspicious afterlife, which was central to both Mithraism and Christianity. Both cults offered their initiates the hope of overcoming earthly mortality, transcending the suffering and finitude of human existence, and achieving a state of bliss in the afterlife. Mithraism promised an ascent of the soul through the planetary spheres and a union with the divine realm of light, while Christianity proclaimed the resurrection of the dead and eternal life in the kingdom of God through faith in Jesus Christ. This concern with salvation and immortality constituted a strong appeal to the inhabitants of the Roman world, seeking comfort in the face of the uncertainty of life and the fear of death, making both cults competitive in offering hope and meaning beyond earthly existence.

Ritual meals, or sacred banquets, were another common feature of both cults, although with specific forms and meanings. Mithraic banquets, held in the dark and mysterious mithraea, symbolized communion and fraternity among initiates, and possibly a symbolic communion with Mithraic deities. The Christian Eucharist, the celebration of Jesus' Last Supper with his disciples, and the sharing of bread and wine as the body and blood of Christ, also represented an act of communion with Christ and unity among believers. Both cults valued ritual meals as a sacred moment of sharing, strengthening community ties, and approaching the divine, although the theological meaning and specific ritual context differed in each case.

Both cults also emphasized the importance of a rigorous ethical and moral code, guiding the conduct of their followers and shaping their character. Mithraism valued virtues such as discipline, loyalty, courage, self-control, and fraternity, promoting an ideal of moral perfection and self-mastery among initiates. Christianity preached love of neighbor, compassion, humility, forgiveness, and justice, proposing an ethical code centered on love for God and neighbor, and on imitating the moral example of Jesus Christ. Although the specific ethical codes differed in some aspects, both cults shared the concern with moral conduct and the ethical transformation of their followers, presenting themselves as ways of life that demanded moral commitment and a pursuit of virtue.

Community dimension and fraternity were equally important in both Mithraism and Christianity. Both cults promoted a strong sense of belonging to a cohesive community, united by common beliefs and practices, and by bonds of fraternity and mutual solidarity. Mithraea, as closed ritual spaces reserved for initiates, created an intimate and familiar environment where members of the cult met regularly, shared mysteries, and strengthened their social ties. Christian communities, organized in local churches, also offered a space for fellowship, mutual support, and spiritual fraternity among believers, providing a sense of belonging and collective identity. Both cults recognized the importance of the social dimension of religion and community support for spiritual growth and the experience of faith.

Finally, in theological terms, both cults presented monotheistic tendencies, although with important nuances. Mithraism, although it maintained a pantheon of auxiliary deities, focused on the figure of Mithras as the supreme deity and orderer of the cosmos, and tended towards a form of henotheism or even monolatry, with primordial worship directed at Mithras, and the other deities subordinated to his power. Christianity, from its Jewish roots, was explicitly monotheistic, proclaiming the existence of a single God, creator of the universe, although with the Trinitarian doctrine introducing a complexity in the understanding of divinity. The emphasis on divine uniqueness, or at least on the primacy of a supreme deity, was a common element to both cults, distinguishing them from more explicitly polytheistic Roman civic religions.

Despite these notable similarities, the differences between Mithraism and Christianity were equally significant and would ultimately be decisive for their divergent historical paths. These differences lay in the origins, theology, ritual practices, social structure, and fundamental message of each cult, outlining two distinct religious paths in the context of the Roman world.

The origins and historical context of the two cults differ substantially. Mithraism emerged from obscure and debated origins, possibly with roots in Persian or Indo-Iranian religious traditions, but configuring itself distinctly in the Roman world, perhaps as a syncretic creation of the imperial period. Christianity, on the other hand, has clearly Jewish origins, arising in the context of first-century AD Palestinian Judaism, and centering on the historical figure of Jesus of Nazareth, whose life, death, and resurrection constitute the foundation of the Christian faith. This difference in historical and geographical origins profoundly influenced the development and characteristics of each cult.

The central figure of each cult also presents fundamental differences. Mithras was a mythical figure, surrounded by mystery and shrouded in complex mythical and iconographic narratives, but without a verifiable historical existence. Jesus Christ, on the contrary, was a historical figure, whose existence and activity in first-century Palestine are attested by historical sources, both Christian and non-Christian, although his divine nature is a matter of faith and theological interpretation. The historical character of Jesus Christ gave Christianity an anchor in earthly reality and a palpability that Mithraism lacked, whose founder remained in the realm of myth and legend.

The mythology of each cult delineated distinct religious narratives. Mithraism focused on the myth of

Tauroctony, the primordial sacrifice of the bull by Mithras, and on other myths associated with the life and deeds of Mithras, constituting a complex and enigmatic mythical cycle, transmitted mainly through iconography and oral tradition. Christianity was based on the biblical narrative, from the Old Testament to the New Testament, with the Gospel narrating the life, teachings, death, and resurrection of Jesus Christ, constituting a linear and narrative sacred history, widely disseminated through written texts and oral preaching. The narrative and accessible nature of Christian mythology, based on written texts and a relatively straightforward story, contrasted with the more mysterious and iconographic character of Mithraic mythology, which required initiation and esoteric interpretation to be fully understood.

The ritual practices of each cult also presented significant differences. Mithraism was characterized by initiation rites in the seven degrees, by secret rituals performed in the dark and mysterious mithraea, by ritual meals, and possibly by hymns and liturgical prayers, constituting a complex and enigmatic ritual system, surrounded by secrecy and reserved for male initiates. Christianity, initially simpler and more accessible in its rites, gradually developed a more elaborate liturgy, centered on the Eucharist, baptism, communal prayer, Scripture reading, and the sacraments, constituting a more open and participatory ritual system, although also with elements of mystery and clerical hierarchy. The secret and exclusively male nature of Mithraic rites contrasted with the more public and universalist character of Christian rites, which influenced their ability to attract and integrate different segments of the Roman population.

The social structure of the two cults also differed. Mithraism seems to have remained a secret and fraternal society of initiates, with a rigid hierarchical structure of seven degrees, and with a predominantly male membership, especially associated with the Roman army and certain professional groups. Christianity, from the beginning, sought to constitute itself as a universal and inclusive Church, open to people of all sexes, social classes, and ethnic origins, with a developing ecclesiastical hierarchical structure, but with a broader and more diverse community base. The more open and universalist social structure of Christianity gave it an advantage in expanding and attracting a larger number of followers, compared to the more restricted and elitist character of Mithraism.

Finally, the fundamental message of each cult presented crucial differences. Mithraism, centered on the myth of Tauroctony and the cult of Mithras as the orderer of the cosmos and guarantor of cosmic order, conveyed a message of strength, discipline, loyalty, and the pursuit of spiritual light, with an emphasis on personal transformation and the ascent of the soul to the celestial realm. Christianity, centered on the figure of Jesus Christ and the message of the Gospel, proclaimed God's love for humanity, the forgiveness of sins through the sacrifice of Christ, the promise of universal salvation, and the importance of love for neighbor and social justice, with an emphasis on divine grace, faith, and compassion. The Christian message of universal love and salvation for all, more accessible and emotionally resonant for many, in contrast to the more austere and esoteric message of Mithraism, contributed to its greater appeal and its success in winning over faithful.

In conclusion, the parallel between Mithraism and Christianity reveals a complex picture of similarities and differences. Both cults, arising in the same historical and cultural context, shared common elements such as the mystical nature, the promise of salvation, ritual meals, rigorous ethics, the community dimension, and monotheistic tendencies. However, the differences in origins, central figure, mythology, rites, social structure, and fundamental message outlined two distinct religious paths, with profound implications for their historical trajectory. These differences, ultimately, contributed to the triumph of Christianity and the gradual decline of Mithraism.

Chapter 26
Mithraism versus Christianity in the Quest for Followers

The coexistence of Mithraism and Christianity in the Roman Empire did not unfold in a sphere of indifference or peaceful coexistence, but rather in a context of intense religious competition, marked by a subtle yet persistent rivalry in the quest for followers. Although historical evidence does not point to widespread violent confrontations between the two cults, the religious dynamics of the time were characterized by an implicit dispute for space, influence, and adherents, where each religion sought to assert its validity, attract new members, and consolidate its position in the Roman religious landscape. This competition and conflict, although not always explicit, shaped the relationship between Mithraism and Christianity, influencing their development, their expansion strategies, and ultimately, their fate in the late Roman world. Analyzing the religious competition between Mithraism and Christianity, unraveling its forms of manifestation, exploring the strategies used by each cult in the quest for followers, and understanding the factors that influenced this dynamic is crucial to understanding the complex religious interaction of the period and the eventual decline of one cult at the expense of the other.

The nature of the competition between Mithraism and Christianity was multifaceted, encompassing different levels and forms of manifestation. It was not a military conflict or a declared religious war, but rather a more subtle and ideological competition, which unfolded in the field of persuasion, preaching, offering religious and social benefits, and the dispute for hearts and minds. The rivalry manifested itself in the search for converts, in attracting new members to each cult, in the attempt to demonstrate the superiority of its doctrine, its morality, and its promise of salvation, and in the quest to consolidate its influence and legitimacy within Roman society.

Religious competition between Mithraism and Christianity was inevitable due to several factors. Firstly, both cults largely competed for the same target audience. Although Mithraism was particularly popular among the military and certain male professional groups, and Christianity initially attracted more of the lower and marginalized social strata, both cults, over time, expanded their appeal to different segments of Roman society, including urban centers, the middle classes, and even some elites. The overlap in potential audiences and the search for new followers created a scenario of natural competition, where each cult sought to stand out and attract those who were undecided or dissatisfied with other religious options.

Secondly, both cults offered answers to similar spiritual and existential needs, sought by many inhabitants of the late Roman world. The promise of personal salvation, life after death, communion with the divine, meaning for life, community support, and an ethical and moral code were central elements of both Mithraism and Christianity, and represented a strong appeal for individuals seeking comfort, hope, and religious guidance in a period of uncertainty and social transformation. Competition in offering religious and spiritual benefits made comparison between the two cults inevitable, and the choice between one and the other depended on various factors, such as the specific message of each cult, personal experience, social influence, and individual context.

Thirdly, the exclusive nature of both cults, albeit with different nuances, contributed to religious competition. Mithraism, as a mystery religion, required restricted initiation and total commitment to its secrets and rites, drawing a clear line between initiates and non-initiates. Christianity, with its message of religious exclusivity, affirmed the uniqueness of God and the singularity of Christ as the only path to salvation, rejecting pagan polytheism and demanding exclusive and total adherence to the Christian faith. This exclusivity, in both cases, created a dynamic of "either/or", reinforcing religious competition and the need to convince the undecided of the superiority of their own path.

The strategies used by Mithraism and Christianity in the quest for followers reflected the distinctive characteristics of each cult and its specific appeal to different segments of Roman society. Mithraism, with its mysterious and esoteric character, attracted followers through mystery and secrecy, the promise of higher knowledge, and an intense and transformative religious experience through initiation. The mysterious atmosphere of the mithraea, the secret rites, the complex symbolic and iconographic language, and the gradual progression through the seven degrees created a sense of exclusivity, privilege, and access to a hidden truth, which could be particularly attractive to individuals seeking a deeper and more engaging religion than traditional civic cults. The fraternal and community aspect of Mithraism, accentuated by sacred banquets and camaraderie among initiates, reinforced the sense of belonging and mutual support within the Mithraic brotherhood, creating strong bonds between members of the cult.

Christianity, on the other hand, used different expansion strategies, centered on open preaching and dissemination of the Gospel message, offering social and welfare benefits, and appealing for personal conversion through faith in Jesus Christ. Missionary preaching, carried out by apostles, bishops, and presbyters, carried the Christian message to different regions of the Roman Empire, reaching a vast and diverse audience. The translation of the Scriptures into Latin and their wide dissemination made the sacred texts accessible to a growing number of people. The practice of charity and assistance to the needy by Christian communities, through the distribution of food, care for the sick, and support for orphans and widows, demonstrated Christian love in action and attracted followers seeking material and spiritual help. The emotional and personal appeal of the Christian message, centered on the figure of Jesus Christ and the promise of divine love and forgiveness, resonated with individual needs and created a strong impulse for personal conversion and adherence to the Christian faith.

The competition between Mithraism and Christianity did not take place in a social and political vacuum, but rather in a specific historical context that influenced its dynamics and outcome. The expansion of Christianity coincided with a period of social transformations, political crises, and religious insecurity in the late Roman Empire, factors that favored the growth of the new cult and challenged the position of pagan religions, including Mithraism. The crisis of traditional Roman values, the loss of confidence in civic institutions, barbarian invasions, civil wars, and epidemics generated a climate of anxiety and uncertainty, leading many individuals to seek comfort, security, and meaning in new forms of religiosity. Christianity, with its message of hope and salvation beyond the earthly world, offered a spiritual refuge and an anchor of faith in a context of instability and change.

Imperial support for Christianity, from the 4th century AD onwards, with the conversion of Constantine and the progressive legislation favorable to Christianity and unfavorable to paganism, represented a decisive factor in the religious competition with Mithraism and other pagan religions. Imperial favor conferred on Christianity a legitimacy and social and political prestige that Mithraism never achieved.

Imperial patronage translated into financial support for the construction of churches, tax exemptions for the Christian clergy, social promotion for Christians, and repressive measures against pagan cults, altering the balance of religious power in the Roman Empire and unequivocally favoring the growth and consolidation of Christianity.

The dynamics of religious competition between Mithraism and Christianity were also influenced by the notions of exclusivity, tolerance, and religious intolerance that characterized the context of the time. Traditional Roman polytheism, characterized by religious tolerance and acceptance of the coexistence of different cults and deities, contrasted with the message of exclusivity of Christianity, which rejected polytheism and proclaimed the falsehood of all other gods. Mithraism, although a mystery religion with rites restricted to initiates, was not necessarily intolerant of other cults, and could coexist with other religious practices within Roman society.

Religious intolerance, which would become a characteristic of dominant Christianity in the late Roman Empire, represented a disadvantage for Mithraism and other pagan religions in religious competition. The progressive anti-pagan legislation issued by Christian emperors, from the end of the 4th century AD onwards, prohibiting pagan sacrifices, closing pagan temples, and persecuting "heretics" and "idolaters", created an environment of growing religious intolerance, which marginalized and repressed pagan cults, including

Mithraism, and unequivocally favored the religious monopoly of Christianity.

In short, the competition and conflict between Mithraism and Christianity in the quest for followers in the Roman Empire was a complex and multifaceted reality, shaped by religious, social, political, and cultural factors. The rivalry between the two cults, although not always violent, played a crucial role in the religious dynamics of the period, with Christianity gradually ascending as a formidable competitor, benefiting from strategic advantages, imperial support, and a favorable historical context, which contributed to the gradual decline of Mithraism and the final triumph of Christianity as the dominant religion of the Roman Empire.

Chapter 27
The Gradual Decline of Mithraism

Despite its considerable popularity and influence in the Roman world during the 2nd and 3rd centuries AD, Mithraism could not resist the rise of Christianity and, from the 4th century AD onwards, began a gradual process of decline, which culminated in its almost complete disappearance from the religious landscape of the Roman Empire at the end of Antiquity. The decline of Mithraism, a complex and multifaceted phenomenon, was not the result of a single factor, but rather a confluence of causes that interacted synergistically to undermine the foundations of the cult, reduce its number of followers, and lead it to historical obscurity. Analyzing the causes of the decline of Mithraism, exploring the factors that contributed to its gradual disappearance, and understanding its final trajectory is essential to complete the picture of the history of Mithraism and to understand the religious dynamics that shaped the late Roman world and the transition to the Middle Ages.

The primary and most decisive factor for the decline of Mithraism was undoubtedly the rise and triumph of Christianity as the dominant religion in the Roman Empire. As explored previously, Christianity emerged as a formidable religious competitor, vying for the same audience, offering alternative answers to the same spiritual and existential needs, and benefiting from strategic advantages, imperial support, and a favorable historical context. The progressive conversion of the Roman elite to Christianity, imperial legislation favorable to Christianity and unfavorable to paganism, and growing religious intolerance on the part of Christian authorities created an increasingly hostile environment for pagan religions, including Mithraism, and increasingly conducive to the expansion and consolidation of Christianity.

Imperial support for Christianity, from the 4th century AD onwards, represented a fatal blow to Mithraism and other pagan religions. The conversion of Emperor Constantine, the issuance of the Edict of Milan (313 AD) which granted freedom of worship to Christianity, and subsequent legislation favorable to Christianity and unfavorable to paganism initiated a process of gradual Christianization of the Roman Empire, which profoundly altered the balance of religious power and marginalized pagan cults. Imperial patronage translated into financial support for the construction of churches, tax exemptions for the Christian clergy, social promotion for Christians, and, most importantly, the withdrawal of state support for pagan cults, and the progressive suppression of their rituals and temples.

Anti-pagan legislation issued by Christian emperors, especially from the end of the 4th century AD onwards, culminating in the decrees of Theodosius I that made Christianity the official religion of the Roman Empire and prohibited pagan worship, represented a frontal attack on paganism and sealed the fate of Mithraism and other traditional religions. The prohibition of pagan sacrifices, the closure and destruction of pagan temples, the repression of pagan ritual practices, and the persecution of "heretics" and "idolaters" created an environment of growing religious intolerance, which marginalized and repressed paganism and favored the religious monopoly of Christianity. Mithraism, as a pagan mystery religion, was directly affected by these repressive measures, losing imperial support, facing the hostility of Christian authorities, and seeing its temples and rituals gradually suppressed.

In addition to direct persecution, Christian religious intolerance created a social climate unfavorable to paganism, discouraging adherence to non-Christian cults, promoting conversion to Christianity, and stigmatizing pagan religious practices as "idolatry", "superstition", and "work of the devil". Polemical Christian preaching, denigrating pagan gods and their cults, and presenting Christianity as the only true and morally superior religion, contributed to the delegitimization of paganism in the public consciousness and to the conversion of many individuals to Christianity, in search of social legitimacy, imperial protection, or religious conviction.

The social structure of Mithraism, although initially a source of strength, may have become a limitation in the long term in the context of competition with Christianity. The restricted and exclusively male character of Mithraism limited its potential for expansion and attraction of a larger number of followers, compared to Christianity, which presented itself as a universal and inclusive religion, open to people of all genders and social classes. The rigid hierarchical structure of seven degrees of Mithraism, although it may have been attractive to certain groups, could also be perceived as excessively complex and demanding for others, compared to the Christian ecclesiastical structure, which was becoming progressively more organized and hierarchical, but maintaining a broader and more accessible community base.

The loss of military support, traditionally a strong suit of Mithraism, may have been another contributing factor to its decline. The gradual Christianization of the Roman army, throughout the 4th century AD, with the conversion of soldiers and officers to Christianity and the promotion of Christian values within the troops, reduced the influence of Mithraism in the military and deprived the cult of a traditional and influential support base. The shift in the center of gravity of the Roman Empire to the East, with the founding of Constantinople and the growing weight of the eastern provinces, where Mithraism had never achieved the same popularity as in the West, may also have contributed to the decline of Mithraism, shifting the geographical focus of power and religious influence to regions less favorable to the cult of Mithras.

The barbarian invasions and the fall of the Western Roman Empire in the 5th century AD represented the final blow to Mithraism and other pagan religions in Western Europe. The political, social, and economic turmoil resulting from the invasions, the fragmentation of the Empire, the destruction of cities and infrastructure, and widespread instability created an unfavorable context for the maintenance and transmission of pagan cults, which were already in decline under pressure from Christianity and imperial legislation. Mithraism, dependent on local community structures and the maintenance of mithraea in urban and military contexts, became particularly vulnerable to the social disorganization and material destruction caused by the invasions.

The disappearance of Mithraism was not an abrupt and sudden event, but rather a gradual process of decline over centuries, with regional and chronological variations. In the 4th century AD, there were already signs of decline in some regions, with the decrease in the construction of new mithraea and the abandonment of some existing sanctuaries. In the 5th century AD, with the barbarian invasions and the fall of the Western Roman Empire, Mithraism practically disappeared from Western Europe, surviving only in some isolated regions of the East and the Byzantine Empire, where it would also eventually be suppressed by dominant Christianity.

The archaeological remains of Mithraism, namely abandoned mithraea, defaced or reused Tauroctony reliefs, and ritual objects scattered throughout museums and collections, bear witness to the decline and gradual disappearance of the cult of Mithras. The silence of Mithraic textual sources, in contrast to the growing vocality of Christian and anti-pagan sources, reinforces the image of a progressively marginalized, silenced, and forgotten cult by history. Mithraism, once a popular and influential cult in the Roman world, became a religion of the past, whose mysteries were lost in the mists of time, leaving us only fragmentary and enigmatic traces to reconstruct its history and understand its legacy.

In conclusion, the decline of Mithraism was a slow and complex process, driven by a confluence of factors, where the rise of Christianity played a preponderant role, but where structural limitations of the cult itself, the loss of military support, the social and political transformations of the late Roman Empire, and growing religious intolerance also contributed. Mithraism, unable to compete with the dynamism and adaptability of Christianity, and to resist the pressure of imperial legislation and Christian hostility, saw its support bases gradually eroded, its number of followers dwindle, and its sanctuaries abandoned or destroyed, thus disappearing from the Roman religious landscape and leaving us only archaeological and iconographic vestiges to unravel its mysteries and understand its role in the religious history of the ancient world.

Chapter 28
The Enduring Legacy of Mithraism

Throughout this detailed exploration of Mithraism, we have traversed the intricate paths of this fascinating mystery cult, unveiling its secrets, analyzing its rites, deciphering its iconography, and understanding its place in the complex religious landscape of the Roman Empire. Having reached this point of conclusion, it is essential to reflect on the enduring legacy of Mithraism, to assess its historical importance, to ponder its cultural impact, and to recognize the marks that this enigmatic cult left on Western civilization, even after its decline and disappearance. Despite having been eclipsed by Christianity and relegated to historical obscurity, Mithraism did not become extinct without leaving a significant trace, with elements of its symbolism, its theology, and its religious experience reverberating, in subtle or more evident ways, in later traditions and in Western culture itself. These final considerations aim to synthesize the legacy of Mithraism, highlighting its most relevant aspects and reaffirming its importance as an object of study and as a testimony to a rich and complex form of religiosity in the ancient world.

One of the most evident legacies of Mithraism lies in the rich and complex iconographic system that the cult developed and which is manifested in the numerous mithraea scattered throughout the Roman Empire. The reliefs of the Tauroctony, the mural paintings, the sculptures of Cautes and Cautopates, the zodiacal cycles, and the vast symbolic bestiary of Mithraism constitute an artistic and iconographic heritage of inestimable value, which continues to fascinate and intrigue scholars, artists, and admirers of ancient culture. The visual language of Mithraism, with its wealth of symbols, allegories, and metaphors, demonstrates the sophistication of Mithraic religious thought and its ability to communicate profound mysteries through image and symbol. The iconographic heritage of Mithraism represents an enduring legacy for the history of art and religion, inspiring diverse interpretations and continuing to challenge our understanding of the ancient world.

Beyond iconography, Mithraism left an important legacy in the field of the history of religions and mystery cults. Mithraism, as one of the most prominent mystery cults of the Roman world, represents a paradigmatic example of this type of religiosity, characterized by initiation, secrecy, transformative experience, and the promise of personal salvation. The study of Mithraism contributes to a broader understanding of the mystery cults of antiquity, revealing their common characteristics, their regional variations, and their reciprocal influences. The comparison of Mithraism with other mystery cults, such as the Eleusinian Mysteries, the Dionysian Mysteries, or the Egyptian Mysteries, allows us to draw parallels, identify shared elements, and understand the diversity and richness of mystery religiosity in the Greco-Roman world.

Mithraism, in its competition and contrast with Christianity, also leaves an important legacy for understanding the religious dynamics of the late Roman Empire and the rise of Christianity. The analysis of the competition between the two cults reveals the strategies of religious expansion, the factors of success and decline, and the complex interactions between different forms of religiosity in a specific historical context. The study of Mithraism as a "failed competitor" of Christianity allows us to better understand the reasons for the triumph of Christianity and the decline of paganism in the Roman world, and to assess the importance of factors such as imperial support, social structure, religious message, and historical context in the trajectory of religious movements.

Although one cannot speak of a "direct influence" of Mithraism on Christianity, the comparison between the two cults reveals parallels and possible indirect influences that deserve to be considered. The date of December 25, traditionally associated with the birth of Mithras and later adopted by Christianity to celebrate Christmas, suggests a possible influence of the Mithraic festive calendar on the fixing of the Christian birth date, although the issue is debated and complex. Some Mithraic symbols and rituals, such as the ritual banquet, the use of light and darkness in the liturgy, and the idea of a hierarchy of initiates, present parallels with elements of Christianity, although the interpretations and specific origins of these parallels are also the subject of debate and speculation. It is important to emphasize that these parallels do not imply a direct "filiation" of Christianity to Mithraism, but rather the existence of a common cultural and religious environment, where ideas, symbols, and religious practices circulated and influenced each other.

Beyond the strict historical and religious context, Mithraism also leaves a legacy in the popular imagination and contemporary culture. The mystery and enigma that surround Mithraism, its secret and esoteric nature, the richness of its iconography, and its complex and fragmentary history continue to arouse the curiosity and interest of readers, artists, and filmmakers. Mithraism inspires works of fiction, historical novels, video games, and documentaries, which explore its mysterious world and its symbolic language, revealing the enduring fascination that the cult of Mithras exerts on the contemporary imagination. This presence in popular culture, although sometimes distorted or romanticized, demonstrates the continuity of interest in Mithraism and its enigmatic heritage.

The study of Mithraism, even in the academic context, continues to be a lively and dynamic field of research, with new archaeological discoveries, new iconographic interpretations, and new theoretical approaches constantly enriching our knowledge of the cult. The continuity of scientific research on Mithraism, through archaeologists, historians of religion, art historians, and philologists, demonstrates the relevance of the cult as an object of study and its ability to arouse the interest and interpretive effort of generations of scholars. The complexity and enigma of Mithraism remain as an intellectual challenge and as an invitation to explore and discover new aspects of this fascinating mystery cult.

In summary, the legacy of Mithraism, although less visible and direct than that of other ancient religions, is real and multifaceted. Its iconographic heritage, its importance for understanding mystery cults, its role in the religious dynamics of the late Roman world, its presence in the popular imagination, and the continuity of scientific research on the cult testify to its historical and cultural relevance. Mithraism, even in its decline and disappearance, leaves us a lasting legacy of mystery, enigma, and fascination, inviting us to explore the secrets of the sacred caves and to unravel the visual and mythical language of one of the most intriguing and enigmatic cults of the ancient world. With these final considerations, we conclude our journey of exploration of Mithraism, hoping to have contributed to a deeper and more appreciative understanding of this fascinating and complex religious phenomenon of the Roman world.

Epilogue

As we conclude this journey through the mysterious world of Mithraism, it is crucial to acknowledge the tireless work of researchers and scholars who, over the centuries, have dedicated themselves to unraveling the secrets of this fascinating cult. Without their passion, rigor, and insight, Mithraism would remain even more obscured by the mists of time, and our understanding of the religious past of the Roman Empire would be incomplete.

Since the Renaissance, with the awakening of interest in classical culture, scholars and antiquarians have focused on the archaeological and textual remains of Mithraism, seeking to reconstruct its history, interpret its symbols, and understand its meaning in the context of the Roman world.

In the 19th century, with the development of archaeology as a scientific discipline, excavations of archaeological sites such as Ostia Antica, Rome, and Carnuntum revealed to the world the richness and complexity of the mithraea, the underground sanctuaries of Mithraism. The discovery of reliefs, murals, sculptures, and ritual objects provided an unprecedented view of the art, rituals, and religious life of the followers of Mithras.

In the 20th century, research on Mithraism intensified, with the publication of monographic studies, the organization of international congresses, and the creation of research centers dedicated to the subject. Franz Cumont, a renowned Belgian historian, stood out as one of the pioneers in the study of Mithraism, with his monumental work "Les Mystères de Mithra" (1894-1900), which laid the foundation for modern research on the cult.

In recent decades, research on Mithraism has expanded and diversified, with the application of new methodologies, the analysis of new archaeological and textual evidence, and the incorporation of interdisciplinary perspectives. Scholars such as Maarten Vermaseren, Roger Beck, Manfred Clauss, and David Ulansey, among many others, have contributed significantly to deepening knowledge about Mithraism, exploring its origins, its theology, its rituals, its iconography, and its impact on Western culture.

Contemporary research on Mithraism covers a variety of areas of study, from archaeology and art history to the history of religions, classical philology, and cultural anthropology. Archaeologists continue to excavate and analyze mithraea in various regions of the former Roman Empire, bringing to light new finds and expanding the map of the cult's presence. Art historians and iconographers dedicate themselves to interpreting the complex visual language of Mithraism, deciphering its symbols, its allegories, and its hidden messages. Historians of religions compare Mithraism with other mystery cults and religions of antiquity, seeking to understand their common characteristics and their specificities. Classical philologists analyze the scarce Mithraic textual sources, seeking to extract from them information about the theology, rituals, and organization of the cult. Cultural anthropologists explore the social and cultural significance of Mithraism, its function in Roman society, and its impact on the construction of individual and collective identity.

The study of Mithraism, however, is not limited to the past. Interest in this mysterious cult transcends the academic sphere, finding resonance in popular culture, contemporary art, and even the spiritual quest of modern man. Mithraism, with its aura of mystery, its rich iconography, and its promise of spiritual transformation, continues to fascinate and inspire, challenging us to question our beliefs, to explore new forms of spirituality, and to seek a deeper meaning for our existence.

By recognizing the legacy of researchers and scholars of Mithraism, we celebrate their passion for knowledge, their dedication to research, and their invaluable contribution to understanding the past. May their work continue to inspire new generations of researchers and illuminate our path in the search for wisdom and truth.

www.ingramcontent.com/pod-product-compliance
Lightning Source LLC
LaVergne TN
LVHW040057080526
838202LV00045B/3681